# ANGELS AND
# MINISTERS OF GRACE

# Angels and Ministers of Grace

An ethno-psychiatrist's
contribution to
biblical criticism

## M. J. Field

Longman

LONGMAN GROUP LIMITED
LONDON

Associated companies, branches and representatives
throughout the world

First published 1971

ISBN 0 582 12662 2

Printed in Great Britain by
William Clowes & Sons, Limited
London, Beccles and Colchester

For C.E.K.H.

With love

# Contents

# Author's acknowledgements

I am grateful for friendly help and criticism bestowed by the following: Dr Rosemary Angel of the Royal Botanic Gardens, Kew; Mr D. C. A. Bradshaw of Winneba Training College; Professor Meyer Fortes of King's College, Cambridge; Dr Gordon Haliburton of the University of Botswana, Lesotho; Dr E. H. Hare of London University Institute of Psychiatry; Mrs Eva L. Meyerowitz; Miss Margaret Munn-Rankin of Newnham College, Cambridge; Professor E. G. Parrinder of King's College, London; Dr C. P. Seager of the University of Sheffield; Dr H. S. Smith of the Department of Egyptology, University College, London; Dr M. F. Tuke of Zambia; and Professor D. Winton-Thomas of Cambridge.

M. J. FIELD

# Preface

This book is not another addition to the hundreds of tons of existing biblical scholarship.

It is an attempt to kindle some illumination by non-scholastic methods.

Three such methods are used.

The first is the application of hypothesis. This is an accepted part of scientific method and is often able to cause disordered masses of recorded fact to fall into comprehensible order.

The second method is the demonstration of identity in kind between certain observable facts of today and certain matter recorded as fact in the biblical narratives. In a working life of some thirty-five years spent for the most part in West African villages as an ethnographer and a clinical psychiatrist, I have become thoroughly familiar not only with certain mental phenomena seldom seen in Europe (such as 'spirit possession') but also with some almost universal primitive customs (such as the control of land by the priestly agents of land-owning deities). On re-reading the biblical narratives, I am now able to recognize many an item of behaviour there recorded as something which I myself have *seen*.

A third method is used in reaching the conclusions regarding the nature of angels and their societies. This is the simple process of collecting together all the scattered information provided by many narratives and examining it as a whole.

For such of my few minor reflections as are purely speculative I do not apologize. Astronomers have speculated freely on the origin of the moon and as yet this is all they can offer. But against a background of relevant knowledge they are entitled to offer it.

I have chosen to quote from the Revised Version of 1884, because this adds to the accuracy without sacrificing (as does the New English Bible) the beauty and vitality of the Authorized Version.

I need hardly say that I share the view that the human figures that people the pages of the Bible did exist. I also believe that they were subject to the same laws of Nature which prevail today and that these were never suspended.

I have been asked by the publisher to add to this preface some account of how the ideas in the book were born.

Some arrived as isolated flashes of illumination when I was engaged in some unrelated and humdrum ploy.

The first of these occurred when I had been in West Africa only about a year. One day I walked twenty-five miles along the beach and arrived at sundown, alone and unannounced, in a fishing village, where I prepared to spend the night on the floor of a dilapidated rest-house. That evening a deputation of elders came to see me. They said, bluntly, that they disbelieved my story that I had walked along the beach—Europeans travelled by car, not on foot—and that they suspected me to have 'come out of the sea' in the manner of some of the forbears who had founded their village.

This was my first intimation that unsophisticated people could more readily accept a supernatural explanation than a prosaic one.

On reflection I also realized that their own founding fathers, said to have emerged miraculously from the sea, had probably arrived exactly as I arrived, and that most myths, particularly origin-myths, were based on sober fact subsequently embellished with supernatural 'explanation'.

Throughout the years other instances of this 'supernatural- ization' process cropped up. In one part of the country I was shown a funnel-shaped hole in the ground, terminating, at the bottom of the funnel, in a tumble-down and clearly ancient, circular drywall leading into a labyrinth of fascinating under- ground passages, water-worn between sandstone strata. From the ceremonial still carried on at the spot I gathered that it had been the principal holy place of the aboriginal inhabitants of the district. At a later point in the local history a party of well- armed, intimidating immigrants arrived and the aborigines fled underground and hid there till starved out. They then emerged and, to the newcomers among whom they subsequently lived peaceably, they became known as 'the tribe that came out of a hole in the ground'. This became an acceptable origin-myth which spread to other districts.

Then there was a time when I was staying in an unbearably hot and humid valley. Most evenings I took a walk to the top of a nearby hill where there was a breath of air. I did not know that the hill was regarded as the home of a local minor deity. As an aid to finding the trail which I had beaten through the tall grass and shrubs I tied to the latter a number of short lengths of white roller-bandage. The villagers, curious as to the meaning of these objects, were afraid to ask me, but deputed a hunter to precede me one day to the hilltop, conceal himself there, and observe my doings. This he did. He reported that I had stood on the edge of the scarp slope of the hill and waved a fan. This was true, for I often carried a palm-leaf fan which I used for swishing away flies and creating a little breeze. The villagers, as I afterwards learned, discussed the ritual of the fan and decided that it was a part of the magical process whereby I obtained my daily bread, for I was obviously not gainfully occupied day by day and had no visible means of support.

Time and again throughout my years in Africa it occurred that a perfectly prosaic happening in which I myself participated was given a supernatural interpretation and it became clear that wherever there was a choice between a miraculous and a mundane explanation the former always won. I am persuaded that this was the disposition, not so markedly of the few who actually participated in biblical events, as of those who knew of them only by embellished hearsay.

It was not till I had known West Africa for more than twenty-five years that pure chance brought illumination concerning the nature of the 'spirit of the Lord' which 'moved' various Hebrew prophets. I was at that time staying in a remote village in (what was then) N.W. Ashanti. I had already seen, over the years, some thousands of cases of 'spirit possession' and knew that the phenomenon was the perfectly natural one of 'dissociation of consciousness'—no more remarkable than the diurnal marvel of sleep. But I had not connected it with Hebrew prophets. Around my Ashanti village at that time there had been almost an epidemic among new shamans of 'running to bush' on the occasion of their initial 'possession'. One evening I was reading, as an aid to language learning, the only piece of literature in the vernacular—the New Testament. When I reached St Mark's account of how the prophet Jesus began his dedicated career by being 'driven of the spirit into the wilderness', it came to me, with the force of a revelation, that such 'driving' was something I had *seen*.

A few days later my cook—a Muslim from the far north— told me of a countryman of his who had run to bush and stayed there five years. Asked what spirit would so possess and drive a Muslim, he replied, 'God took him.' I recognized this as the exact phrase used in the story of Enoch: 'And Enoch walked with God and he was not, for God took him.'

When I next had a spell of leisure I re-read the Bible in the light of African experience and found that a large body of Hebrew prophets and early Christian converts conformed to the familiar pattern of 'spirit possession'—an age-old, world-wide pattern persistently exhibited wherever society allows people to behave naturally.

During this process of re-reading the Bible, it struck me that the 'two angels', also described as 'three men' and as 'the Lord', who visited both Abraham and Lot, partook of hearty meals, washed their feet and aroused the lusts of the Sodomites, could not have been other than mortal men. This led me to collect together all the scattered accounts of other angels. It became clear that there must have been several distinct orders of venerated holy men (or God's 'messengers') and that each group betrayed *some* features which I had met in real life. Even the Assyrian/Babylonian/Persian group, which had some quite unfamiliar traits, were nevertheless recognizable as herbalists. That they administered a powerful hallucinogenic drug to a favoured few was made clear to me not as an ethnographer but as a physician. The disagreeable *side-effects* of this drug were its striking tell-tale feature—giddiness, buzzing in the ears, prostration, depression, and a sense of utter desolation. One recipient appears to have had two drugs, the second inducing a spell of wakefulness with intense mental activity and clarity.

Orthodox commentators long ago remarked that in the early Old Testament narratives it is often difficult to distinguish between the Angel of the Lord and the Lord himself. It is but a short step from this to the realization that human angels were not the only lordly men whom posterity came to confuse with the Almighty. This confusion no doubt had two causes. The earliest was the primitive taboo on the utterance of the divine name, with the substitution of titles also applicable to earthly lords. The later factor was the officious editing of scripts by scribes who, in their anxiety to present the patriarchs as the Almighty's favoured intimate associates, uttered the divine name all too freely when transcribing tales of the doings and sayings of human lords. That editors must needs edit is no idle speculation. There is no writer who does not know what darkening of truth their 'improvements' can wreak. H. G. Wells has somewhere stated that there is no human passion so compelling as the urge to alter what someone else has written.

No sooner had I grasped that the angel of the Lord and all too often (though not, of course, always) the Lord himself were flesh and blood, than two other solid human figures, both familiar to ethnographers, emerged from the mist of super-naturalized tradition. One was the powerful landlord on whose territory humble migrants settled, ritual blessing was necessary and whose curse devastating to successful husbandry. The Lord God of the garden of Eden was no doubt such a land-lord till he fell into the hands of pious editors. The other was the inconspicuous priestly agent (or angel) of the land-owning deity into whose domain powerful migrants moved.[1] This was the rather furtive nocturnal man to whom the immigrant Jacob 'wept and made supplication' in his anxiety to elicit the all-important blessing.

M. J. FIELD

[1] West African anthropologists will recognize the *asasewura*, the *tendana*, and the *shikpong-wulomo*, the *zigba-wono* and others.

# Part I

# SOME FUNDAMENTAL CONCEPTS

# 1 The Name of the Lord

The first task of this essay is to offer a simple hypothesis which, if accepted, transforms great wastes of unedifying myth into sober chronicle.

This proposition is that in the earliest biblical accounts of ancestral deeds the term 'the lord' refers sometimes to the Lord God of Heaven and sometimes to a landlord or some other respected human being. In the minds of the actual participators in events, there was of course no confusion between the God whom they worshipped and the chieftain to whom they were subject, but in posterity's versions of forebears' doings ambiguity must have arisen.

The first cause of this confusion was the ancient taboo on the utterance of the divine name. Substitute words meaning lord, master, or landowner, equally applicable to human beings, were used.[1]

Later, when scribes converted the orally transmitted stories into written records, another truth-obscuring process began—that of editing scripts in the light of a more coherent monotheism. Later still, when the primitive taboo had relaxed, the divine name itself was no doubt often boldly substituted by officious editors for lords who were originally mortal men. For the later scribes, insistent on the God-given superiority of the Hebrews to all other men, every mortal landlord or priestly land-agent who had conversed with patriarchs on such matters as land tenure became the Lord God of Heaven.

An example of one myth which this hypothesis converts into a basically credible chronicle is that of the Garden of Eden. The lord of that story, who becomes in the edited versions the Lord God, is a human landlord of some substance. His angel, or

[1] The eminent Hebrew scholar, Professor D. Winton-Thomas, tells me that no one knows for certain the meanings of Elohim, Adonai, El, Shaddai, Yaweh and Baal.

messenger, is a human servant armed with a burnished sword. (Nearly all polished steel swords and chariots of the Old Testament are described as flaming or fiery.) The basic story is that of the origin, not of mankind, but of Abraham's lineage. We are given a careful genealogy of this lineage and there is no reason to doubt its truth, though there may be some omissions:

Adam – Seth – Enos – Cainan – Mahalaleel – Jared – Enoch – Methuselah – Lamech – Noah – Shem – Arphaxad – Salah – Eber – Peleg – Reu – Serug – Nahor – Terah – Abraham.[2]

Among illiterate people there is nothing more carefully accurate than family trees and family traditions when these are passed down by intelligent elders whose duty it is to know them. These men are like our own small children in that they will not tolerate the smallest variation in an oft-told tale. On the other hand, there is nothing more wildly inaccurate than the hearsay and rumour bandied about by outsiders, one of whose delights is to adorn a simple story with supernatural or stereotyped embellishments.[3]

Adam thus becomes a solitary farming settler of a kind familiar to most rural people in such countries as West Africa. Possibly he is a fugitive from tribal justice. He settles on fertile land somewhere near the Euphrates by permission of the local landowner. He is instructed not to molest a certain sacred tree. (Most tribes have sacred trees.) The landlord is benevolent and walks in Adam's garden in the cool of the evening. He is concerned that Adam has no wife and gives him a woman help of a class 'meet' for him. We may guess that she is a slave-girl and in concealment of this fact a supernatural origin is later fabricated for her. It may well be that she did tempt Adam into tasting the sacred fruit which perhaps she had heard was ceremonially eaten at the puberty rites in which youths were initiated into the tribal rules of 'good and evil'.

[2] Genesis 11:10–27.
[3] The serpent is a widespread embellishment of origin myths.

When Adam turned out untrustworthy and sacrilegious, he was naturally expelled and kept out at the point of a sword. His descendants did not, apparently, move far away, for Noah was near the Euphrates at the time of the great flood which buried the city of Ur, and Abram was still in the region of Ur when he began his recorded adventures.

Adam's son Cain was also a tiller of the ground and seemingly tilled it by favour of a landlord, to whom he naturally brought an annual tribute in kind—a very common custom in many regions to this day. Cain was expelled by the landlord for murdering the brother whose gift of livestock inevitably found more favour in the eyes of the overlord than did Cain's gift of mere vegetables. The landlord did not, however, entirely withdraw his overlord's protection from Cain, for he set upon him a 'mark', which was probably a tattooed or cicatrized facial tribal mark of the kind familiar to many tribes even now.[4]

[4] Genesis 4:2–16.

# 2 The Landlord and his Settlers

So much Old Testament narrative concerns migration and settlement that we must piece together such scattered fragments of information as we are incidentally given concerning the rules of land tenure and the allocation of land to settlers.

Much illumination is cast upon this topic by a consideration of similarities in existing unsophisticated societies. Some widely-held ideas of these societies about the supernatural relationship between man and the land that he uses are of vital importance to understanding.

The history of West Africa, for instance, has much to teach us here, for it is a history of innumerable migrations and settlements. There is hardly a village of any size that does not consist of several 'quarters', each representing a separate settlement. Furthermore, the process is inconspicuously going on today and its details can still be observed.

There are many types of migration but only two that we need to consider here.

The first is that of a single migrant or a very small, weak party of migrants settling by permission on land already controlled by a larger, stronger group. The headman or chief of, say, a Volta-side community, after describing his domain to the inquiring ethnographer, may add, 'We also have a party of [say] Dahomey farmers [or Fante fishermen] living on our land. They pay us an annual sheep. We are glad to have them there because our own numbers are small and they help us in time of trouble— a big flood or a big fire. In the old days of warfare they would have helped in driving off an enemy attack.'

This kind of immigrant is anxious to respect such local rules as the observance of the weekly day of rest of the land-owning deity, the weekly day of fishing prohibition or the day on which water may not be drawn from the local sacred water supply. (All water supplies are venerated.) Furthermore, on the settler's arrival the landlord performs a small ritual—a libation or the sacrifice of a fowl—and commends the newcomer to the care of the local gods of the land. Without this blessing the stranger cannot hope to work the land without disaster. The operative power attributed to ritual blessing and ritual curse cannot be exaggerated.

Even when the land is sold for such uses as cocoa farming, the seller carries out a handing-over ritual when he gives the buyer necessary information and commends him to the care of the land-deities.

Such a settler was Adam, whose story, shorn of subsequent supernatural accretions, is very ordinary. When Adam is thrown out for misbehaviour the landlord does that which only land-lords can do: he calls down the landlord's curse on any attempt by Adam to cultivate the land. 'Cursed is the ground for thy sake; in toil shalt thou eat of it all the days of thy life; thorns also and thistles shall it bring forth to thee; and thou shalt eat the herb of the field. In the sweat of thy face shalt thou eat bread.'[1]

Similarly, when Cain's landlord throws him out for murder-ing the brother whose payment-in-kind was better received than Cain's own, he gives him the much-dreaded landlord's curse of the failure of crops. It is this that Cain regards as 'too hard to bear'. 'And the Lord said unto Cain . . . And now cursed art thou from the ground . . . When thou tillest the ground it shall not henceforth yield unto thee her strength.'[2]

We are not told how far afield these descendants of Adam settled, evidently not far, for it is clear that down to the days of Noah they were still worried about the curse on their agriculture. 'And Lamech . . . begat a son and he called his name Noah, saying, this same shall comfort us for our work and for the toil of our hands, because of the ground which the Lord hath cursed.'[3]

[1] Genesis 3:17, 18, 19.
[2] Genesis 4:11, 12.
[3] Genesis 5:28, 29.

The lord who curses can only be a landlord, not the deity. Deities do not curse: they implement human curses.

It is also quite clear that there were two peoples in Noah's region: the landlord's tribe—tall, well set-up men—and the immigrants. Furthermore, it is plain that there was some inter-marriage. 'And it came to pass, when man began to multiply on the face of the ground, and daughters were born unto them, that the sons of God[4] saw the daughters of men that they were fair; and they took them wives of all that they chose. And the Lord said, My spirit shall not strive with man for ever, for that he also is flesh . . . The Nephilim [giants] were in the earth in those days, and also after that, when the sons of God came in unto the daughters of men, and they bare children to them: the same were the mighty men which were of old, the men of renown.'

The lord could hardly have made it clearer that both he and the immigrants were made of 'flesh'.

Noah 'found grace in the eyes of the Lord' and it may well be that the Lord told him that the countryside had a history of big floods and warned him to be prepared.[5]

There is a second type of migration and settlement which must be considered. This is the reverse of Adam's. It is the entry of a more powerful people—powerful either by numbers or by arms—into the sparsely inhabited territory of a weak unorganized landowner. There are innumerable instances of this in many tribal histories and the same basic principles are everywhere observed.

In such a situation the powerful immigrants never molest the aborigines. It is of cardinal importance to have their goodwill, for they know all the necessary land ritual and how to invoke

---

[4] The New English Bible changes this into 'sons of the gods'. My own mentors, however, assure me that there is no textual justifi-cation for this change. As I see it, 'God' here simply means the landlord.

[5] The archaeological evidence, beginning with Woolley's well-known work in Ur from 1922 to 1934, indicates that there were at least nine big floods in Iraq and that one of them could have been Noah's. M. E. L. Mallowan, 'Noah's Flood Reconsidered', *Iraq*, vol. XXVI, 1964.

the favour or disfavour of the local land-gods, sprites, and other invisible powers. A bullying newcomer who outraged the aborigines' rights could not hope to live on the land without disaster. Trees would fall on him, wild animals attack him, floods overwhelm him, lightning strike his house, blight devastate his crops, barrenness close up the wombs of his wives, and mortal sickness end his own unhappy life. He cannot afford to offend the gods of the land by injuring the established old servants on whose ritual blessing every newcomer is dependent.

Wherever we go, therefore, we find that a priest of the aboriginal section of the community is the nominal overlord of the land. Such priests are seldom members of an exalted family: they are often—except on one day of the year—not distinguishable from the humblest tiller of the soil. But annually, the grand political chief of the community doffs his grandeur and brings the ceremonial head a bundle of firewood or some other symbol of submission, and in return receives his ritual blessing. Often it is difficult to discover the obscure but vitally important man who annually 'does the custom for the land', for most of the common people do not even know who he is. But the chief knows him and would not offend him, though he is not always willing to point him out. It sometimes happens that the ethnographer's first clue to the importance of this lowly man is the sight of him being carried shoulder-high in the place of honour in some annual procession.

It is quite certain that the principle of the dependence of powerful migrants on the goodwill of the gods of the conquered inhabitants was recognized by the Assyrians as late as the days of Shalmanezer. We are told that the Israelites were conquered and carried away captive and that the conquerors settled their own people in Samaria. But because these strangers were ignorant of the correct local land ritual they were plagued by lions and sometimes killed. 'They knew not the manner of the God of the land.' They therefore laid their plight before the king of Assyria and the king duly commanded, 'Carry thither one of the priests whom ye brought from thence; and let them go and dwell there, and let him teach them the manner of the God of the land. So one of the priests whom they had carried away from Samaria came and dwelt in Beth-el, and taught them how they should fear the Lord.'[6]

[6] 2 Kings 17:23–28.

# 3 The Ultimate Ownership of Land

We have gathered, or at least been led strongly to suspect, that people permanently settled on a land were regarded by later arrivals as the operative owners and that the newcomers were in fealty to them and, through them, to the land gods. The goodwill of those able to invoke either the bane or blessing of those gods was essential to newcomers.

We may further gather that the land of well-established occupants could be bought and sold. Abraham bought land from the children of Heth for Sarah's burial place and the famine-stricken peasants of Egypt sold their land to Pharaoh in the days of Joseph.

But of the grazing rights of unoccupied land by nomadic peoples and of the settlement of migrants on such lands we are told nothing outright and must therefore piece together fragments picked up here and there.

After brooding over these fragments, which will be exhibited to the reader one by one in due course, I wish to submit the hypothesis that the *ultimate* owner of the land was the universal supreme Sky God.

A digression into the universal nature of the Sky God is called for here.

Most, if not all, primitive peoples, however polytheistic, believe in a supreme Sky God or Rain God, the creator of heaven and earth, the giver of life and the giver of power to all other gods. Usually he is regarded as aloof, indifferent to the petty needs of men, and as having delegated a great measure of power to lesser gods. The lesser gods are very often impressive works of nature—mountains, volcanoes, rivers, lakes and so on. Still smaller gods of specialized interests, such as war gods and fertility goddesses, are innumerable.

But here and there the Sky God is more approachable. We find, for instance, that the aboriginal Guan inhabitants of Ghana had a Sky God named Bereku or Bleku, whose worship must have been well organized, for his name is still preserved in many widely scattered place names—Berekum, Berekuso or Blekuman—'the place of Bereku'.

Among Abraham's neighbours his friend Melchizedek, the king of Salem, was a priest of the 'God Most High'.[1] The Egyptian Amenhotep IV of the 18th Dynasty, about 1375 BC, changed his own name to Akhnaton and worshipped only Aton, the Egyptian Supreme Sky God, who certainly existed before Amenhotep's time.[2] As we shall see later, the God of Heaven, as conceived in Babylon and in Persia, did much to elevate Hebrew theology during the captivity.

There is no suggestion anywhere in the Old Testament that the Hebrews and their neighbours shared the widespread belief that the earth was a great goddess fertilized by the rain—the semen of the Sky God. But there is a good deal of suggestion that the *ultimate* owner of all land was the universal supreme Sky God. He is often referred to as the 'Possessor of Heaven and Earth' and is reported as saying, 'The land shall not be sold in perpetuity; for the land is mine; for ye are strangers and sojourners with me.'[3]

---

[1] Genesis 14:18, 19.
[2] Arthur Weigal, *The Life and Times of Akhnaton*, London, 1923; Cyril Aldred, *Akhenaten*, London, 1968.
[3] Leviticus 25:23.

# Part II

# THE OLD
# TESTAMENT
# ANGELS

# 4 The Angel as Land Agent

Having submitted the hypothesis that the universal Most High God was the ultimate owner of all land, I wish to submit a further hypothesis. I suggest that 'the Angel of the Lord' (often loosely referred to as 'the Lord' or even as 'God'), whose conversations with the migrant patriarchs were almost always on the subject of land allocation, was the Sky God's priestly land agent—some obscure little man whose co-operation and ritual blessing immigrants were passionately anxious to secure.

In regard to 'angels', although it is true that 'the heavenly host' and various ethereal 'ministering spirits' were also called angels, and that they often appeared to people in dreams and 'visions of the night', the biblical word for angel in both Hebrew and Greek simply means a *messenger* and the most convincing biblical accounts of angels endow them with all the attributes of flesh and blood.

Abram's dealings with 'the Lord' begin with a talk with what seems to be a land agent in Ur of the Chaldees. One may suppose that Abraham consults this official about land hunger, perhaps over-grazing, around his birthplace, and is advised that there is a better hope of prosperity if he goes to Canaan. Furthermore, the land agent promises him the necessary blessing.

'Now the Lord said unto Abram, Get thee out of thy country, and from thy kindred, and from thy father's house, unto the land that I will show thee . . . And I will bless them that bless thee, and him that curseth thee will I curse.'[1]

Abraham departs, reaches Sichem, where he meets the land agent again and is given details of where to settle. 'And the

---

[1] Genesis 12:1, 3.

Lord appeared unto Abram and said, Unto thy seed will I give this land: and there builded he an altar unto the Lord who appeared unto him. And he removed from thence unto the mountain on the east of Beth-el and pitched his tent, having Beth-el on the west and Ai on the east: and there he builded an altar unto the Lord, and called upon the name of the Lord.'[2] He settles and in due time becomes 'very rich in cattle, in silver and in gold'.

But there is trouble with his nephew Lot, who also 'had flocks and herds and tents'. 'And the land was not able to bear them, that they might dwell together: for their substance was great, so that they could not dwell together: and there was a strife between the herdmen of Abram's cattle and the herdmen of Lot's cattle.'[3]

They settle the dispute amicably and Abraham moves out to the plain of Mamre, a friendly Amorite. This contract is presumably between Abraham and Mamre. The Sky God's land agent is not involved. Then there is warfare between the Amorites and some other neighbours and the wealthy Abram is able to put 318 fighting men, 'servants, born in his own house', into the field.

It seems that any ruling made by God's land agent was resignedly accepted by rival land-seekers. 'And it came to pass at that time that Abimelech spake unto Abram, saying, God is with thee in all that thou doest.' Abimelech and Abram then make a solemn covenant together to see that their herdmen also observe the ruling.[4]

From time to time during the rest of his life, Abram has dealings with other angels, but as these appear to be of a quite different order of holy men, unconnected with land tenure, we will postpone examination of them until we have discussed the land-agent angels who deal also with Abram's son and grandson.

After the death of Abraham, his son Isaac is afflicted by famine and proposes to move to Egypt, but God's land agent

[2] Genesis 12:7, 8.
[3] Genesis 13:6, 7.
[4] Genesis 21:22–34.

offers him other land and gives him the much-coveted blessing. 'And the Lord appeared unto him and said, Go not down into Egypt: dwell in the land which I shall tell thee of: sojourn in this land and I will be with thee and will bless thee: for unto thee and unto thy seed I will give all these lands: and I will establish the oath which I sware unto Abraham thy father . . . And Isaac departed thence and encamped in the valley of Gerar, and dwelt there.'[5]

But there is trouble with competitors. 'And the herdmen of Gerar strove with Isaac's herdmen, saying, The water is ours; and he called the name of the well Esek, because they contended with him. And they digged another well and they strove for that also, and he called the name of it Sitnah. And he removed from thence and digged another well and for that they strove not, and he called the name of it Rehoboth, and he said, For now the Lord hath made room for us and we shall be fruitful in the land. And he went up from thence to Beer-sheba.'[6]

As soon as he arrives in Beer-sheba he has another interview with the Lord, who wastes no time but comes to see him 'the same night'. Isaac is reassured and given the sought-after blessing 'for Abraham's sake'. The rival herdmen actually *see* the Lord with Isaac, witness the placing of the boundary stone and accept the ruling without further demur.

'Then Abimelech went to him from Gerar and Ahuzzath his friend, and Phicol the captain of his host. And Isaac said unto them, Wherefore are ye come unto me, seeing ye hate me and have sent me away from you? And they said, *We saw plainly* that the Lord was with thee: and we said, Let there now be an oath betwixt us, even betwixt us and thee, and let us make a covenant with thee: That thou wilt do us no hurt, as we have not touched thee, and as we have done unto thee nothing but good and have sent thee away in peace: thou art now the blessed of the Lord.'[7]

Isaac's son Jacob goes off to work for his mother's brother Laban and stays there till he has acquired wives, a considerable

[5] Genesis 26:2, 3, 17.

[6] Genesis 26:20-23.

[7] Genesis 26:26-29.

body of children, 'cattle, maidservants and menservants, camels and asses'. Laban and his sons become hostile, so he decides to migrate. On the journey his party is threatened by his old enemy Esau, the brother whom he had cheated out of his birthright. He is filled with concern for his wives and children. But there is also a mysterious man who disputes his right to enter the territory.

'And he rose up that night, and took his two wives and his two handmaids and his eleven children, and passed over the ford of Jabbok. And he took them and sent them over the stream and sent over that he had. And Jacob was left alone; and there wrestled a man with him until the breaking of the day. And when he saw that he prevailed not against him, he touched the hollow of his thigh; and the hollow of Jacob's thigh was strained as he wrestled with him. And he said, Let me go, for the day breaketh. And he said, I will not let thee go, except thou bless me. And he said unto him, What is thy name? And he said, Jacob. And he said, Thy name shall be called no more Jacob, but Israel: for thou hast striven with God and with men, and hast prevailed. And Jacob asked him, and said, Tell me, I pray thee, thy name. And he said, Wherefore is it that thou dost ask after my name? And he blessed him there.'[8]

In Genesis this assailant is called a man: in Hosea he is called an angel.[9] Three things are to be noticed about him. First, the immense importance that Jacob attaches to his blessing: Hosea says that Jacob 'wept and made supplication to the angel'. Second, that the angel refuses to give his own name—a characteristic of other angels which we shall meet later in this study. Third, that he gives Jacob a new theophorous name, pertaining to Elohim, the possessor of Heaven and Earth.

Later Jacob comes to Shalem, a settlement in Shechem, and pitches his tent. There is a city there and Jacob *buys* land. 'And Jacob came in peace to the city of Shechem, which is in the land of Canaan, when he came from Paddan-aram; and encamped before the city. And he bought the parcel of ground, where he

[8] Genesis 32:22–29.
[9] Hosea 12:4.

had spread his tent, at the hand of the children of Hamor, Shechem's father, for an hundred pieces of money.'[10]

Later still, however, the angel (here loosely called God) turns up again and tells Jacob to go and live in Bethel and set up a land-mark there.[11] Jacob obeys, the Lord joins him there, blesses him, reminds him that his name is now Israel, and says, 'The land which I gave unto Abraham and Isaac, to thee I will give it and to thy seed after thee will I give the land. And God went up from him in the place where he spake with him. And Jacob set up a pillar in the place where he spake with him, a pillar of stone: and he poured out a drink offering thereon and poured oil thereon. And Jacob called the name of the place where God spake with him, Beth-el.'[12]

Thereafter Jacob 'dwelt in the land of his father's sojournings, in the land of Canaan'[13] and, so far as we know, had no more dealings with 'the Lord' on the subject of land tenure.

[10] Genesis 33:18–19.
[11] Genesis 35:1.
[12] Genesis 35:12–15.
[13] Genesis 37:1.

# 5 The Angel as Man of God

We have considered those angels or messengers of God who dealt with the needs of migrating patriarchs in the matter of the allocation of territory. It appears likely that such angels were the priestly land agents of the universal Sky God who was the ultimate owner of all land—the 'Possessor of Heaven and Earth'. As we have noted, it is common practice among primitive peoples to regard the land as owned by some god or other and to seek the co-operation of some politically negligible priestly servant of that god, whose ritual blessing is essential to any settler's prosperity.

But there are other kinds of angel who appear from time to time throughout the Bible beginning with Abram.

Such angels are indisputably human beings: they eat a good square meal, wash their feet and sometimes bring satisfaction to forlorn women who have failed to bear children to their own aged husbands. Some of them are recognizable as angels at sight, perhaps by reason of tattooed or cicatrized faces, 'circumcised lips', or some distinctive clothing or hairdressing. Some passages suggest that, like priests, they often wore linen as did 'the man Gabriel' in the Book of Daniel. When they were given bread, this was unleavened. When recognized they always inspired reverence, awe, fear, and, in evil-doers, terror. One man who encountered an angel was stricken with hysterical dumbness, a batch of others with blindness and another with a briefly paralysed hand. Some angels, however, were not recognized as such till they had worked some 'wonder', often involving fire, suggesting that they might have been the forerunners of the Persian *magi* or *pyrethes*. The angel of the Lord that came up from Gilgal to Bochim was visible to 'all the children of Israel' and after listening to a speech that he made they were all reduced to abject and noisy blubbering.

Such angels contrast sharply with those ethereal ones that appeared in visions, flying around the throne of heaven, mingling with six-winged beasts, seven-horned lambs, golden candlesticks, trumpets, fire, blood, and cities encircled with jewelled walls.

The angels who, one gospel tells us, were found at the empty tomb of Jesus, are in others simply called 'two men' and 'a young man', and they delivered a straightforward message about Jesus having gone to Galilee. The 'young men' who visited Abram on their way to Sodom were presumably the same 'angels' who turned up a little later at the house of Abram's nephew Lot in Sodom itself and there aroused the lusts of the Sodomites.

Human angels are sharply distinguished from prophets, who are usually noisy conspicuous men of local origin, denouncing local wickedness and loudly crying in public against the depravity of the times. Angels are self-effacing, elusive holy men, usually itinerant, turning up unexpectedly and making off precipitately. They were never, so far as we know, 'moved by the spirit' in the histrionic manner of many prophets. They quietly rebuked evildoers and encouraged disheartened good men. They gave advice, help, blessing and food when needed. They seem to have been quietly observant of what went on in the lay community and probably informed one another. A few of them appear to have been hermits living in the wilderness: possibly these wilderness dwellers represent a separate order of holy men, but perhaps they all observed periods of solitary retreat.

Though the behaviour of the Old Testament angels suggests that they were members of an international religious secret society—more secret than the Rechabites and less secret than the Essenes—the important thing about them is that they not only worshipped the universal Most High God, but they may well have been the originators of monotheism. It has been suggested that Moses acquired monotheism from the Pharaoh Akhnaton. He may have done so, but Akhnaton was probably not the first monotheist. It is likely that the Egyptian desert was only one of the deserts in or around the Arabian Peninsula which bred, by spontaneous generation, a scattered international body of monkish men,[1] often living as hermits, whose first-hand religious experience under the numinous night sky implanted in them not only the idea of the supremacy of the Sky God but the feeling of direct communion with him and the consequent conviction that all other gods were negligible.

That the desert has this quality is well known. C. S. Lewis relates that after one of his lectures on Christianity, an ex-soldier in the audience rose and told him that all his ideas about God and the son of God were worthless and added, 'It isn't that I don't believe in God—I do, because I've experienced him out in the desert.'

Angels were always addressed as 'my Lord'. This provides another field for that confusion which arose in the traditions and scripts between the Lord God and certain eminent human beings. Even highly orthodox biblical commentators have remarked, 'In some of the earlier accounts the angel of Jehovah is hardly to be distinguished from Jehovah himself.'[2] It seems, indeed, that the terms 'the angel of the Lord', 'the Lord' and 'God' were used interchangeably.

We may now examine some Old Testament angels one by one one.

### Abram's angels

We have already discussed those angels who were the Lord's land agents and had dealings with Abram in the matter of land tenure. We now turn to Abram's dealings with another kind of holy man and we are given a very firmly drawn picture, full of vitality and colour, of those who visited Abram on the plain of Mamre and Lot in Sodom.

'And the Lord appeared unto him [Abram] by the oaks of Mamre, as he sat in the tent door in the heat of the day: and he

---

[1] Christian monasticism certainly began in the Egyptian desert and it is likely that it was only copying a much older practice.

[2] Buckland and Lukyn Williams, *The Universal Bible Dictionary*, London, 1914.

lift up his eyes and looked, and lo, three men stood over against him: and when he saw them, he ran to meet them from the tent door and bowed himself to the earth, and said, my Lord, if now I have found favour in thy sight, pass not away, I pray thee, from thy servant: let now a little water be fetched and wash your feet and rest yourselves under the tree: and I will fetch a morsel of bread and comfort ye your heart; after that ye shall pass on, forasmuch as ye are come to your servant. And they said, So do, as thou hast said. And Abram hastened into the tent unto Sarah and said, Make ready quickly three measures of fine meal, knead it and make cakes. And Abram ran unto the herd and fetched a calf tender and good, and gave it unto the servant: and he hasted to dress it. And he took butter and milk and the calf which he had dressed, and set it before them and he stood by them under the tree and they did eat.' The angels then inquire about Abram's barren wife, Sarah, and promise to return again and make her pregnant. This they do and she bears Abraham a son in his old age.[3]

It must be remembered that it is not unknown in the Arabian peninsula for hospitality to include access by the guest to the bed of the host's wife.[4] So it may well be that one of the young men achieved what the aged Abram could not. It must also be remembered that Abram's lineage was grossly inbred. Sarah, for instance, was Abram's half-sister.[5] The male members seem to have been more fertile with concubines than with their official wives and the wives more fertile with angels than with their husbands. And there remains the possibility that concubines had more freedom of movement than wives and thus more opportunity to be made pregnant outside the patriarch's tent.

Abram's angel guests went on to Sodom. 'And the two angels came to Sodom at even: and Lot sat in the gate of

---

[3] Genesis 18:1–8; 21:1, 2, 5.

[4] 'But in old Arabia the husband was so indifferent to his wife's fidelity that he might send her to cohabit with another man to get himself a goodly seed; or he might lend her to a guest.' Robertson Smith, *Kinship and Marriage in Early Arabia*, London, 1903.

[5] Genesis 20:12.

# INBREEDING IN THE LINEAGE OF ABRAHAM[6]

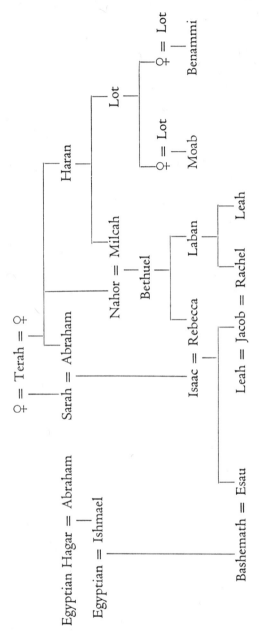

[6] W. H. R. Rivers, *Social Organisation*, London, 1932.

Sodom: and Lot saw them and rose up to meet them: and he bowed himself with his face to the earth; and he said, Behold now, my lords, turn aside, I pray you, into your servant's house, and tarry all night, and wash your feet, and ye shall rise up early and go on your way. And they said, Nay, but we will abide in the street all night. And he urged them greatly; and they turned in unto him and entered into his house; and he made them a feast, and did bake unleavened bread and they did eat. But before they lay down, the men of the city, even the men of Sodom, compassed the house round, both young and old, all the people from every quarter: And they called unto Lot and said unto him, Where are the men which came in to thee this night? Bring them out unto us that we may know them. And Lot went out unto them to the door and shut the door after him. And he said, I pray you, my brethren, do not so wickedly. Behold now, I have two daughters which have not known man; let me I pray you bring them out unto you and do ye to them as is good in your eyes: only unto these men do nothing, forasmuch as they are come under the shadow of my roof.'[7]

Here again, sexual access to any woman member of a man's household is a small matter when set against the honour of a distinguished guest. We learn later that the daughters both had husbands who were present, but these also apparently acquiesced without demur.

The story of Lot proceeds: 'But the men [the angels] put forth their hand and brought Lot into the house to them and shut to the door. And they smote the men that were at the door of the house with blindness, both small and great, so that they wearied themselves to find the door.'[8] It would seem that as soon as the angels emerged into full view of the Sodomites they were at once recognized as members of some awe-inspiring order of holy men.

It was shortly *before* the fruitful visit of the angels to Sarah that Abram had a very long conversation with 'the Lord' and was instructed in the necessity for himself and his household of circumcision (an Egyptian custom, one indication that this

[7] Genesis 19: 1–8.
[8] Genesis 19: 10–11.

angel belonged to an international order). Abram was then, we are told, ninety-nine years old. At this long interview Abram is instructed to change his wife's name and arrangements for her pregnancy are made. When all the circumcisions are completed, including that of Abram himself and the boy Ishmael, the house, being now unpolluted, may be entered by the holy men and they visit Abram and complete the provision for Sarah's pregnancy.[9] The birth of Isaac evidently occurs a year after the multiple circumcisions, for Abraham is then aged a hundred.[10]

The story of Abraham's abandonment of his resolve to sacrifice his son Isaac suggests that there was collusion between two angels, anxious to wean Abraham from the practices of Molech-worship.[11] The first (chronicled as 'God') tells Abraham exactly where to go to carry out this act: the second, who may well have been a hermit, intervenes to stop it. 'And they came to the place which God had told him of: and Abraham built the altar there, and laid the wood in order, and bound Isaac his son and laid him on the altar, upon the wood. And Abraham stretched forth his hand and took the knife to slay his son. And the angel of the Lord called unto him out of Heaven and said, Abraham, Abraham: and he said, Here am I. And he said, Lay not thy hand upon the lad, neither do thou any thing unto him, for now I know that thou fearest God, seeing thou hast not withheld thy son, thine only son, from me. And Abraham lifted up his eyes, and looked and, behold, behind him a ram caught in the thicket by his horns: and Abraham went and took the ram and offered him up for a burnt offering in the stead of his son.'[12]

---

[9] Genesis 17:1–27.

[10] Genesis 21:1–5.

[11] The Semitic Phoenicians who inhabited city states (Tyre, Sidon, Byblos etc.) on the Lebanon coast from 3000–2000 BC caused their children 'to pass through the fire to Molech' which was, in fact, sacrifice in the manner which Abraham proposed for Isaac. Much later than Abraham the Israelites had still to be forbidden to do this. A. N. Whitehead has pointed out that the gifted and advanced Carthaginians were still sacrificing their children to Molech in the days of Plato.

[12] Genesis 22:9–13.

This angel did not, so far as we are told, show himself, but only shouted from some overhead vantage point, perhaps the cave in a cliff-face in which he lived. It may well be that the ram belonged to him. Perhaps the important part of this story is that the angel, being a thorough-going worshipper of the Most High God, was anti-Molech, from whose cardinal rite of child-sacrifice Abraham had not emancipated himself.

*Hagar's angel*

Another angel of Abraham's time, whose presence is wholly credible and whose advice was sane, was the one who met Abraham's pregnant concubine Hagar, who was fleeing from the ill-treatment of the jealous Sarai. 'And the angel of the Lord found her by a fountain of water in the wilderness, by the fountain in the way to Shur. And he said, Hagar, Sarai's hand-maid, whence camest thou? and whither goest thou? And she said, I flee from the face of my mistress Sarai. And the angel of the Lord said unto her, Return to thy mistress, and submit thy-self under her hands.'[13] Any holy man living in the wilderness would certainly have frequented some water source.

A similar story is related of Hagar and her adolescent son Ishmael at the time of the weaning of Isaac. Here again the angel is found beside a well, where presumably he was living a hermit's life. 'And the child grew and was weaned, and Abraham made a great feast on the day that Isaac was weaned. And Sarah saw the son of Hagar the Egyptian which she had borne unto Abraham, mocking. Wherefore she said unto Abraham, Cast out this bondwoman and her son: for the son of this bond-woman shall not be heir with my son, even with Isaac, and the thing was very grievous in Abraham's sight on account of his son.' Abraham discusses the matter with 'God', who in this context seems to have been an angel, and is advised to give way to Sarah but not to grieve, for all will be well. Abraham duly provides Hagar with food and a bottle of water and turns her out with her fourteen-year-old son. When the water is all spent

[13] Genesis 16:7–9.

and she is in despair, another angel shows her a well. She and her son settle in the wilderness of Paran, presumably in a cave. (Paran means the place of caves.) 'And God was with the lad and he grew; and he dwelt in the wilderness and became an archer. And he dwelt in the wilderness of Paran: and his mother took him a wife out of the land of Egypt.'[14]

It seems likely that the statement 'God was with the lad' refers to the angel and means that the latter, who also lived in the wilderness, gave fatherly help.

There is no evidence that Abraham, Isaac and Jacob ever sought more than gross material prosperity. This makes it the more refreshing to contemplate the contemporary existence of unworldly men of God.

### Did Rebecca consult an angel?

During the lives of Isaac and Jacob we hear virtually nothing of the Lord except in his capacity of land agent, but there is one incident that arouses curiosity. When Rebecca is pregnant and feels undue 'struggling' going on in her womb, she goes to 'inquire of the Lord'.[15] Where did Rebecca go and to whom? Was there some shrine or little temple, similar to those at which so many West African supplicants address that kind of inquiry? Did she go to Egypt? Or did she go to some hermit-angel who was also a physician and herbalist, as were certain other angels whom we shall encounter later? At any rate, the Lord diagnosed twins and turned out to be right.

### Moses's angels

Moses as a prophet we shall consider elsewhere. We are at the moment concerned only with his encounters with angels.

The first of these meetings occurs on Mount Horeb, the holy mount of the volcano-god Jehovah, no doubt the haunt of a great

[14] Genesis 21:8-21.
[15] Genesis 25:22.

many holy men and pilgrims. We do not know exactly where Horeb was but it must certainly have been on the eastern seaboard of the Gulf of Akaba, which is volcanic and is adjacent to Midian. The angel who met Moses there appears to have been one of Jehovah's proselytes, anxious to convert Moses to the worship of Jehovah and anxious that he should bring the children of Israel to Horeb and there convert them also. He says, 'When thou hast brought forth the people out of Egypt, ye shall serve God upon this mountain.'[16] On a later occasion he (or some colleague proselyte) explains that Jehovah had not been known to Abraham, Isaac and Jacob.[17]

It is not clear why the existing Jehovah worshippers required the Israelites as allies. It has been suggested that small Israelitish migrations out of Egypt had been going on for a long time and that one batch of such migrants, settled near Horeb, needed allies before they could attempt to enter Canaan. This is highly likely. Most migrations are carried out piecemeal and it is only much later that historians simplify the slow process into one big operation.

The long interview on Horeb between Moses and the angel (who is also referred to as the Lord and as God) begins with the burning bush. This may have been a volcanic phenomenon— Horeb was very active at that time—or may have been one of the fire-magics, with which some angels, prophets and holy men were wont to enhance their prestige. Gideon's angel performed a fire-magic[18] and so also did the prophet Elijah on Mount Carmel.[19] So too do various *dunsini* in Ashanti today. I have found heaps of spent carbide on the ground after some of their fire-magics. What is astonishing about the spectators of signs

---

[16] Exodus 3:12.

[17] Exodus 6:3. It seems likely that the identification of the new volcano-god Jehovah with the universal Sky God was a later editor's attempt to mitigate what he rightly felt to be a retrograde step. The account of the Israelites' initiation into Jehovah worship at the Mount leaves no doubt that the new god of Israel was the volcano itself.

[18] Judges 6:21.

[19] 1 Kings 18:33–38.

and wonders is their eagerness to be deceived and their neglect to take the most elementary precautions against deception. Elijah's barrels of 'water', 'licked up' by the fire, may well have been shale-oil and the twelve 'stones' which were also consumed could have been oil-shale or some rock resembling Kimmeridge coal.[20]

At any rate, Moses's angel did not allow him to investigate closely. 'And the angel of the Lord appeared unto him in a flame of fire out of the midst of a bush: and he looked, and, behold, the bush burned with fire, and the bush was not consumed. And Moses said, I will turn aside now and see this great sight, why the bush is not burnt. And when the Lord saw that he turned aside to see, God called unto him out of the midst of the bush and said, Moses, Moses, and he said, Here am I. And he said, Draw not nigh hither, put off thy shoes from off thy feet for the place whereon thou standest is holy ground.'[21]

It seems possible that when this angel, asked his name, gave it as 'I am that I am', he was only preserving the customary anonymity of angels. [22] Some were positively rude when asked their names. It also seems likely that when he said 'Certainly I will be with thee' he was undertaking to go with Moses to the court of Pharaoh. He evidently knew that court, for he taught Moses a conjuring trick which was also known to Pharaoh's magicians.[23] Later, when Moses has various conferences with 'the Lord' in Egypt itself, it seems probable that the same angel was present and was his adviser.

But before Moses gets to Egypt, on his way there he encounters another angel, a homicidal fanatic obsessed with the importance of circumcision for Moses's son. (Every religious movement is liable to have a lunatic fringe.) 'And it came to pass on the way at the lodging place, that the Lord met him, and sought to kill him. Then Zipporah took a flint, and cut off the

---

20 Professor Parrinder has drawn my attention to a secret sacred fire involving naphtha. 2 Maccabees 1.

21 Exodus 3:2-5.

22 I do not wish to stress this as I am aware that 'Yahweh' has been thought to have a similar meaning.

23 Exodus 7:10, 11.

foreskin of her son, and cast it at his feet, and said, Surely a bridegroom of blood art thou to me. So he let him alone: then she said, A bridegroom of blood art thou to me, because of the circumcision.'[24]

There may well have been a considerable band of angels taking part in the enterprise of getting the Israelites out of Egypt. One of them takes a message to Aaron. 'And the Lord said to Aaron, Go into the wilderness to meet Moses. And he went, and met him in the mountain of God, and kissed him.'[25] It seems likely that several angels who knew the wilderness well acted as guides, using smoke signals and lights. 'And the Lord went before them by day in a pillar of cloud, to lead them the way; and by night in a pillar of fire, to give them light; that they might go by day and by night ... And the angel of God which went before the camp of Israel removed and went behind them; and the pillar of cloud removed from before them and stood behind them.'[26]

'Behold, I send an angel before thee, to keep thee by the way, and to bring thee into the place which I have prepared. Take ye heed of him and hearken unto his voice; provoke him not, for he will not pardon your transgression: for my name is in him.'[27]

'And now go, lead the people unto the place of which I have spoken unto thee: behold, mine angel shall go before thee.'[28]

## Balaam's angel

The angel who had an encounter with the prophet Balaam at the time of the immigration of the Israelites into Moabite country appears as a resident of the country and a very staunch upholder of the same god as Balaam's god. This god was not the god of Balak the king of Moab, who followed Baal. Since Moabites and Midianites were descendants of Lot and Abraham

[24] Exodus 4:24–26.
[25] Exodus 4:27.
[26] Exodus 13:21; 14:19.
[27] Exodus 23:20, 21.
[28] Exodus 32:34.

respectively,[29] Balaam's god was no doubt the Most High, the god of Abraham, and his angel was friendly towards the Israelite immigrants. The angel story goes as follows.

The elders of Midian and Moab were sent by Balak the king to Balaam 'with the rewards of divination in their hand' and urged him to invoke the curse of his god upon the immigrants, Baal being competent to deal only with his own children. Balaam consulted the Lord, who replied, 'Thou shalt not curse the people, for they are blessed.' Balak sent a second delegation, saying, 'I will promote thee unto very great honour and I will do whatsoever thou sayest unto me: come therefore, I pray thee, curse me this people.' Again Balaam refused but he invited the elders to stay the night and consented to go and see Balak next morning. He set off. 'Now he was riding upon his ass and his two servants were with him . . . Then the angel of the Lord stood in a hollow way between the vineyards, a fence being on this side and a fence on that side. And the ass saw the angel of the Lord and she thrust herself unto the wall and crushed Balaam's foot against the wall and he smote her again. And the angel of the Lord went further and stood in a narrow place where was no way to turn . . . Then the Lord opened the eyes of Balaam and he saw the angel of the Lord standing in the way, with his sword drawn in his hand: and he bowed his head and fell on his face. And the angel of the Lord said unto him, Wherefore hast thou smitten thine ass these three times? Behold, I am come forth for an adversary, because thy way is perverse before me: and the ass saw me and turned aside before me these three times: unless she had turned aside from me, *surely now I had even slain thee* and saved her alive. And Balaam said unto the angel of the Lord, I have sinned; for I knew not that thou stoodest in the way against me: now therefore, if it displeases thee, I will get me back again. And the angel of the Lord said unto Balaam, Go with the men but only the word that I shall speak unto thee, that thou shalt speak. So Balaam went with the princes of Balak.'[30]

[29] Genesis 19:36, 37; 25:1–4. I Chronicles 1:32, 33.
[30] Numbers 22:24–35. The italics are the author's.

The narrative goes on to relate that Balaam stood his ground and not only refused to curse the Israelites but blessed them. No doubt he bore in mind that an angel who had avowed a first intention of killing him with a sword was capable of resuming that intention.

## Joshua's angels

We have one other instance of what seems to have been an armed angel in Canaan at the time of the Israelites' arrival and he explicitly said that he was captain of an armed body belonging to 'the Lord'. Whether they were a permanently armed order of holy men or whether they armed only for the invasion we shall probably never know. 'And it came to pass, when Joshua was by Jericho, that he lifted up his eyes and looked, and, behold, there stood a man over against him with his sword drawn in his hand, and Joshua went unto him and said unto him, Art thou for us, or for our adversaries? And he said, Nay, but as captain of the host of the Lord am I now come. And Joshua fell on his face to the earth and did worship, and said unto him, What saith my Lord unto his servant? And the captain of the Lord's host said unto Joshua, put off thy shoe from off thy foot; for the place whereon thou standest is holy. And Joshua did so.'[31]

Another very authoritative angel met the immigrant Israelites at Boachim. 'And the angel of the Lord came up from Gilgal to Bochim, and he said, I made you to go up out of Egypt and have brought you unto the land which I sware unto your fathers; and I said, I will never break my covenant with you. And ye shall make no covenant with the inhabitants of this land; ye shall break down their altars: but ye have not hearkened unto my voice: why have ye done this? Wherefore I also said, I will not drive them out from before you; but they shall be as thorns in your sides, and their gods shall be a snare unto you.

[31] Joshua 5 : 13–15.

And it came to pass, when the angel of the Lord spake these words unto all the children of Israel, that the people lifted up their voice and wept. And they called the name of that place Bochim: and they sacrificed there unto the Lord.'[32] It is not possible to judge whether he was a local land agent or whether he belonged to the body of angels who instigated the whole migration.

### Gideon's angel

Gideon is 'beating out wheat in the wine press to hide it from the Midianites' when an angel visits him and gives him a mandate to lead a campaign against these oppressors. The visitor is recognized as someone important, for Gideon addresses him as 'my Lord', but it is not till he has performed a fire-magic that Gideon realizes that he is an angel.[33]

### Manoah's angel

Manoah's angel, in common with Abraham's angels on the plain of Mamre, brought pregnancy to a grieving barren woman. The child borne by this woman is, on the angel's instructions, consecrated from the womb and becomes a prophet. Like Moses's angel and Gideon's, Manoah's angel carried out a fire-magic, whereby his angel status was made indubitable, though it had already been noticed that he had a 'very terrible' angel's face. He also refused to give his name, declaring that it was a name of wonder.[34]

It must be remembered that a man in Manoah's position may be himself under the stigma of infertility, and if he suspects his wife's child to have been begotten by an itinerant holy man he

[32] Judges 2:1–5.
[33] Judges 6:11–21.
[34] Judges 13:2–24.

will not say so. I have met such a situation in West Africa, where to be taunted with infertility may make a man commit suicide. A childless African widower married a comely but gadabout young wife, who in due time presented him with a well-favoured child. This child was clearly the offspring of a European. The husband stressed that the child was an albino, which he certainly could not genuinely have believed. He told me that albinism cropped up from time to time among Africans and that no one knew its cause.

## Elijah's angels

The angel who succoured the fugitive prophet Elijah with a pitiably frugal meal seems to have been one of the wilderness-dwellers and, with his endearingly brief speeches, is the only homely figure in that stupendous story. Elijah had had a whole day of nerve-racking competition with four hundred and fifty prophets of Baal before an assembly of 'all the children of Israel' on Mount Carmel, he had defeated them and had then taken them to the brook Kishon and slain the lot. His rain-making ceremonial had been crowned with success and in a tremendous downpour of rain he had run in front of King Ahab's chariot from Carmel to Jezreel, some thirty miles. There he had found that Ahab's wife, Jezebel, was after him and he had fled for his life some ninety miles to Beersheba and left his servant there. 'But he himself went a day's journey into the wilderness and came and sat down under a juniper tree: and he requested for himself that he might die; and said, It is enough, now, O Lord, take away my life; for I am not better than my fathers. And he lay down and slept under a juniper tree and, behold, an angel touched him and said unto him, Arise and eat. And he looked and, behold, there was at his head a cake baken on the coals and a cruse of water: and he did eat and drink and laid him down again. And the angel of the Lord came again the second time and touched him and said, Arise and eat, because the journey is too great for thee, and he arose and did eat and drink and went in the strength of that meat forty days and forty nights unto Horeb the mount of God [another 200 miles].'[35]

It may well be that one reason why Elijah made this pilgrimage to Horeb was to ask the advice of the angels who were always to be found there and probably dwelt in caves like the one in which Elijah lodged. At any rate 'the Lord' who conversed with him in the cave told him to anoint Hazael and Nimshi as kings of Syria and Israel respectively and Elisha as his own successor.

There was at least one other occasion when Elijah accepted instructions from an angel who told him exactly what to do and say. King Ahaziah, who was sick, consulted Baalzebub of Ekton instead of the God of Israel. The angel instructs Elijah to go and rebuke the sick king and tell him that God's displeasure will cause him to die.[36]

### Eli's angel and Jeroboam's angel

Remembering that the angel name Gabriel simply means Man of God, we are entitled to wonder whether several other 'men of God', who appear suddenly and quickly disappear, belong to the order of angels. Among these is the one who came and rebuked Eli for the lecherous behaviour of his sons.[37] There is another anonymous 'man of God out of Judah' who suddenly arrived on foot at Bethel to denounce king Jeroboam for sacrificing to a golden calf that he had set up.

'And Jeroboam was standing by the altar to burn incense . . . And it came to pass, when the king heard the saying of the man of God which he cried against the altar in Beth-el, that Jeroboam put forth his hand from the altar, saying, Lay hold on him. And his hand, which he put forth against him, dried up, so that he could not draw it back again to him . . . And the king answered and said unto the man of God, Intreat now the favour of the Lord thy God and pray for me, that my hand may be restored

[35] 1 Kings 19:4–8.
[36] 2 Kings 1:2–17.
[37] 1 Samuel 2:22, 27.

to me again. And the man of God intreated the Lord, and the king's hand was restored him again and became as it was before. And the king said unto the man of God, Come home with me and refresh thyself, and I will give thee a reward. And the man of God said unto the king, If thou wilt give me half thy house I will not go in with thee, neither will I eat bread nor drink water in this place: for so was it charged me by the word of the Lord, saying, Thou shalt eat no bread nor drink water, neither return by the way that thou camest. So he went another way and returned not by the way that he came to Beth-el.'[38]

If this man of God is admitted into the category of angels, it gives (as will appear later) a total of three whose presence provoked hysterical disablement in the persons they visited. Why these quiet holy men, who never, so far as we are told, presented the impressive spectacle of spirit possession,[39] should have carried such a terrifying aura is at first perplexing. It is less so when it is remembered that they were careful to appear very seldom and always to be anonymous. They avoided creating that familiarity which breeds contempt. It is not what is known about a venerated man that creates fear but his penumbra of unrevealed mystery. In this connection I recall the president of a secret society of medicine-men in West Africa years ago. He was a friend of mine and sometimes took me with him into the bush gathering medicinal herbs, and on one occasion he took me to a meeting of his society at which, needless to say, no secrets were revealed. One day when we returned from herb-gathering I took him home to my fishing-village quarters to give him a drink. As I had no assistant or servant, I called in a friendly young fisherman from next door to serve the drink in ceremonial fashion. To my surprise he consented only with reluctance and I noticed that he trembled and spilt the drink. Afterwards, thinking that he might have been shivering with malaria, I went to offer him remedies. He said, 'Oh, no, I am not sick, but to come so near to that wonderful man made my legs go weak with fear.' I have no doubt that if the herbalist had

[38] I Kings 13:1, 4, 6–10.
[39] See Chapter 7.

pointed a finger at him and said sternly, 'You will be dumb for the rest of today', this would have come to pass.

## David's angel

It will be recalled that whenever there was a devastating pestilence, such as that which destroyed Sennacherib's army in one night ('and when they arose early in the morning, behold, they were all dead corpses'), this was described as the work of an angel of the Lord. Needless to say no one ever saw such an angel. But at the time of David's pestilence, which killed seventy thousand men, there may have been a tangible angel around, not, of course, causing the epidemic but benevolently carrying out a ritual to assist in its decline.

'And the angel of the Lord stood by the threshing-floor of Ornan the Jebusite. And David lifted up his eyes and saw the angel of the Lord stand between the earth and the heaven, having a drawn sword in his hand stretched out over Jerusalem: then David and the elders, clothed in sackcloth, fell upon their faces.' David inquires whether the pestilence is God's punishment for his own sin, and asserts that he and not the innocent populace should pay the penalty. The angel then orders David's seer, Gad, to tell David to go and build an altar on Ornan's threshing-floor. David goes, whereupon Ornan and his four sons, who are threshing wheat, all see the angel. The sons hide in terror and Ornan prostrates himself before David. David builds an altar and prepares a sacrifice which is consumed upon the altar by a fire magic. The angel then sheathes his sword. David wishes to go to a high place at Gibeon to 'inquire of God', but cannot because he is afraid of the angel's sword.[40]

Against the possibility that this angel was a human being are two facts. First, that the angel stood between the earth and the heaven and may therefore have been a cloud, resembling, like Hamlet's cloud and Rorschach's blots, whatever the spectator

[40] 1 Chronicles 21:14–30.

had in mind. Second, that the man whom the angel 'commanded' was Gad, who, as a professional seer, may have divined the command by whatever mode of divination he usually practised.

# 6 The Assyrian– Babylonian–Persian Group of Angels

For many centuries imperial power in the Middle East swayed between Assyria and Babylonia. Sometimes an Assyrian and sometimes a Babylonian king claimed to be King of the World.

The relatively barbaric Israelites, living on the route between Sidon and the Red Sea, were naturally among the pawns in this game. Their resistance was further weakened by the fact that after the death of Solomon they quarrelled among themselves and split into two kingdoms, Judah to the south, consisting of only one tribe with its capital at Jerusalem, and Israel to the north, composed of all the other tribes.

In about 721 BC, Sargon II (Shalmaneser) 'carried Israel away unto Assyria and placed them in Halah and in Habor, on the river of Gozan and in the cities of the Medes'.[1] About 586 BC, Nebuchadnezzar similarly carried off Judah to Babylon, where they stayed for more than two generations. They returned, a much more civilized people, after the conquest of their captors by Cyrus, the founder of the Persian Empire. The Israelites in Assyria never returned and became lost to history.

The period of these captivities gives us our best picture of angels as an international secret society of itinerant holy men, worshipping only the Most High. Some, perhaps all, probably dwelt for a period as hermits in the wilderness, for manna is referred to as 'angels' bread'.[2] They practised austerity, charity and medicine and were given to sermonizing and theological discourse. From them we hear for the first time the doctrine of the immortality of the soul with some overtones of pre-destination and the doctrine of the approaching end of the

[1] 2 Kings 17:6.
[2] 2 Esdras 1:19.

40

world. We hear also of the son of God—God being the Most High—though the idea of the lesser gods having earthly sons was well known, particularly in Egypt, where the kings were sons of the Sun and other deities.

There seems to have been an inner ring of seven archangels who had a set of seven ceremonial names which were passed on to succeeding members for at least 700 years. Michael appears to have been the president, with his headquarters in Persia.[3] Others whose names occur in the captivity narratives were Gabriel (which name simply means Man of God), Raphael and Uriel. They appear to have renounced their ordinary names, but one narrative of the period gives us the only biblical example of an angel who did not flatly refuse to disclose his when asked.

There was also, it seems, an outer ring of associate members and we are given graphic accounts of the gruelling initiation which they underwent. We are told that the prophet Malachi was 'called also an angel of the Lord',[4] though his own short book shows no sign of this.

We may now consider the captivity angels one by one.


### Tobit's angel

Though the book of Tobit is dismissed by commentators as 'fiction' or 'a religious novel', on the assumption that angels were human beings it becomes not only credible but highly illuminating.[5] It gives us a picture of the daily life of an archangel as he appeared to the ordinary people among whom he moved. Apparently he kept his membership of the society a secret and wore no distinguishing uniform.

Tobit, an obsessively righteous Israelite of the tribe of Naphthali, was carried captive to Nineveh by the Assyrians.

[3] Daniel 10:13.

[4] 2 Esdras 1:40.

[5] The book in its present form probably dates from about 250 BC and was always a literary unity. There seems no reason why its writer should not have had access to a document prepared by the conscientious, literate Tobit.

He and his fellow-captives were well treated: his nephew became the king's steward and overseer of the royal accounts: Tobit himself also found 'grace and favour' and became the king's 'purveyor'. Later he became blind through a 'whiteness' in the eyes and at the time of our narrative is in straitened circumstances, supported by his wife Anna, who 'did take in women's works to do'.

One day Tobit decides to send his son Tobias to collect a debt from a kinsman, Gabael in Media, but first sends him out to find a guide for the journey. 'Therefore when he went to seek a man, he found Raphael that was an angel. But he knew not, and he said unto him, Canst thou go with me to Rages? and knowest thou those places well? To whom the angel said, I will go with thee and I know the way well, for I have lodged with our brother Gabael.'[6] Tobias brings the stranger in to his father, who asks for his name and tribe. At first he rudely refuses to reveal this but, mollified by the old man's gentle courtesy, he says, 'I am Azarias, the son of Ananias the great and of thy brethren.'

This is the only biblical example of an angel consenting to disclose his genealogical name.

Tobias and the angel, together with 'the young man's dog', set out on their journey. They camp for the night on the bank of the Tigris. There they catch a fish and roast it for supper. Azarias, who is evidently a physician, makes Tobias save the heart, liver and gall, because the gall was a good cure for 'whiteness' in the eyes, and a smoke made of the liver and gall could cure anyone vexed by 'a devil or an evil spirit'.

Next they lodge with Tobit's cousin, who has a daughter Sara, whom Tobias would marry were she not afflicted with a highly improbable evil spirit. They make a medicinal smoke by taking 'the ashes of perfume' and laying upon them the heart and liver of the fish. The evil spirit flees 'unto the utmost parts of Egypt', Tobias and Sara are united and are given fourteen days of wedding festivity, while Azarias goes on alone and completes the original errand in Media. He rejoins Tobias and they return

[6] Tobit 5:4-6.

to Nineveh, bringing the new wife. On arrival Tobias anoints his blind father's eyes with the fish gall. 'And when his eyes began to smart he rubbed them; and the whiteness peelled away from the corners of his eyes, and when he saw his son, he fell upon his neck.'[7] There are further rejoicings, after which Tobias suggests that his father give brother Azarias a generous fee. It is not clear whether he accepts the money, but he explains that it is God who should be thanked. Then he confesses, 'I am Raphael, one of the seven holy angels.' Tobit and Tobias fall on their faces in awe. Raphael instructs them to record the happening in writing, and when they rise to their feet again, he has made off. As Tobit is literate and meticulously conscientious, we may be sure that his record is as accurate as he could make it. He knew of The Rages happenings only by hearsay.

### Esdras's angel

Esdras, as he is described to us in the Apocrypha, was a scribe 'very ready in the law of Moses' and it was he who negotiated with King Artaxerxes in Babylon for the return of the Jews to their homeland. He organized the migration and, later, the rebuilding of Solomon's temple, and the ruthless expulsion of a large number of foreign wives. He is spoken of as a 'prophet' and he made at least one pilgrimage to Horeb, the Mount of God, where he received 'a charge of the Lord'.[8] Whether this was given to him by a Babylonian angel we are not told, though we know that Horeb was the haunt of angels in much earlier days.

The second book of Esdras, ostensibly written by himself in the first person,[9] gives us a very important and vivid picture of

---

[7] It is possible that the rubbing dislocated a lens. The cure of cataract blindness by lens dislocation is sometimes achieved by primitive medicine-men.

[8] 2 Esdras 2:33.

[9] I am aware that the literature associated with the name of Esdras has a complex history, and that no biblical scholar would agree that the book, as we have it, came straight from the hand of Esdras

the initiation of a candidate into heavenly wisdom and gorgeous visions by an archangel. It is hardly possible to doubt that he is given some hallucinogenic drug. He explicitly states that the angel 'caused him to fall into many trances'.[10]

Esdras's initiation takes place in Babylon. The angel who steered him through this horribly trying time was named Uriel. It is not always clear from Esdras's account of his own experiences whether he was alseep or awake, but it is likely that he himself was uncertain.

He begins his narrative disjointedly with a description of a vision which the angel interprets in the light of the doctrine of immortality—not hitherto a Jewish tenet. 'I Esdras saw upon the mount Sion a great people, whom I could not number, and they all praised the Lord with songs. And in the midst of them there was a young man of a high stature, taller than all the rest, and upon every one of their heads he set crowns, and was more exalted; which I marvelled at greatly. So I asked the angel and said, Sir, what are these? He answered and said unto me, These be they that have put off the mortal clothing and put on the immortal and have confessed the name of God: now are they crowned and receive palms . . . Then the angel said unto me, Go thy way, and tell my people what manner of things, and how great wonders of the Lord thy God, thou hast seen.'[11]

The next chapter tells how Esdras lies 'troubled' on his bed and is filled with fear and a sense of desolation. The angel Uriel is present[12] and answers his perplexities. 'Then answered I and said, I beseech thee, O Lord, let me have understanding: . . . Then answered he me and said, The more thou searchest, the more thou shalt marvel; for the world hasteth fast to pass away, and cannot comprehend the things that are promised to the

himself. I am, however, convinced that it must have been faithfully copied from the first-hand account of someone who had undergone the experiences described.

[10] 2 Esdras 10:28.

[11] 2 Esdras 2:42–45, 48.

[12] 2 Esdras 4:1.

righteous in time to come.'[13] Esdras inquires, 'May I live, thinkest thou, until that time ? or what shall happen in those days ? He answered me and said, As for the tokens whereof thou askest me, I may tell thee of them in part; but as touching thy life, I am not sent to shew thee; for I do not know it.'[14]

Again and again throughout his initiation Esdras experiences deeply distressing fear, depression and physical weakness, and is sustained by the angel. 'Then I awaked, and an extreme fearfulness went through my body and my mind was troubled, so that it fainted. So the angel that was come to talk with me held me, comforted me, and set me up upon my feet.' At one point the angel warns him that he will experience giddiness and buzzing in the ears. 'So he answered and said unto me, Stand up upon thy feet and hear a mighty sounding voice. And it shall be as it were a great motion but the place where thou standest shall not be moved.'[15]

'And in the second night it came to pass that Salathiel the captain of the people came unto me, saying, Where hast thou been ? and why is thy countenance so heavy ? Knowest thou not that Israel is committed unto thee in the land of their captivity ? Up then, and eat bread, and forsake us not, as the shepherd that leaveth his flock in the hands of cruel wolves. Then I said unto him, Go thy ways from me and come not nigh me. And he heard what I said, and went from me. And so I fasted seven days, mourning and weeping, like as Uriel the angel commanded me. And after seven days so it was, that the thoughts of my heart were very grievous unto me again and my soul recovered the spirit of understanding and I began to talk with the Most High again.'[16]

One night when Esdras has heard a voice describing how the world will come to an end to the sound of a trumpet, the angel prescribes further fasting. 'And when he talked with me behold, I looked by little and little upon him before whom I

---

[13] 2 Esdras 4:22, 26, 27.
[14] 2 Esdras 4:51, 52.
[15] 2 Esdras 6:13, 14.
[16] 2 Esdras 5:14–22.

stood. And these words said he unto me: I am come to shew thee the time of the night to come. If thou wilt pray yet more and fast seven days again, I shall tell thee greater things by day than I have heard. For thy voice is heard before the Most High, for the Mighty hath seen thy righteous dealing, he hath seen also thy chastity which thou hast had ever since thy youth. And therefore hath he sent me to shew thee all these things and to say unto thee, Be of good comfort and fear not . . . And it came to pass after this, that I wept again, and fasted seven days in like manner, that I might fulfil the three weeks which he told me. And in the eighth night was my heart vexed within me again, and I began to speak before the Most High. For my spirit was greatly set on fire and my soul was in distress.'[17]

Uriel tends Esdras assiduously night after night, and reassures him when, sorely afflicted with a sense of sin, he asks, 'For what profit is it unto us if we be promised an immortal time, whereas we have done the works that bring death?'[18]

It is not always clear from Esdras's account whether it is the angel or the Almighty who is talking to him, but the instructions concerning procedure are clearly from the angel. 'Nevertheless, if thou wilt cease yet seven days more (but thou shalt not fast in them, but go into a field of flowers, where no house is builded, and eat only the flowers of the field; taste no flesh, drink no wine, but eat flowers only): And pray unto the Highest continually, then will I come and talk with thee. So I went my way into the field which is called Ardath, like as he commanded me; and there I sat among the flowers and did eat of the herbs of the field and the meat of the same satisfied me. After seven days I sat upon the grass, and my heart was vexed within me, like as before.'[19]

Then follows a vision of a mourning woman. 'And behold, suddenly she made a great cry, very fearful: so that the earth shook at the noise of the woman. And I looked and, behold, the woman appeared unto me no more, but there was a city builded

[17] 2 Esdras 6:29–33, 35–37.
[18] 2 Esdras 7:49.
[19] 2 Esdras 9:23–27.

and a large place shewed itself from the foundations: then I was afraid and cried with a loud voice and said, Where is Uriel the angel, who came unto me at the first ? for he hath caused me to fall into many trances and mine end is turned into corruption, and my prayer to rebuke. And as I was speaking these words, behold, he came unto me and looked upon me. And, lo, I lay as one that had been dead and mine understanding was taken from me: and he took me by the right hand and comforted me, and set me upon my feet, and said unto me, What aileth thee ? and why art thou so disquieted ? and why is thine understanding troubled, and the thoughts of thine heart ? And I said, Because thou hast forsaken me and yet I did according to thy words and I went into the field and, lo, I have seen, and yet see, that I am not able to express. And he said unto me, Stand up manfully and I will advise thee. Then said I, Speak on, my Lord, in me, only forsake me not, lest I die frustrate of my hope. For I have seen that I knew not and hear that I do not know. Or is my sense deceived, or my soul in a dream ? Now therefore I beseech thee that thou wilt shew thy servant of this vision. He answered me then and said, Hear me, and I shall inform thee and tell thee wherefore thou art afraid: for the Highest will reveal many secret things unto thee.'[20]

The angel interprets this vision and adds, 'For I knew that the Highest would show this unto thee ... For thou art blessed above many other and art called with the Highest, and so are but few. But tomorrow at night thou shalt remain here; and so shall the Highest shew thee visions of the high things, which the most High will do unto them that dwell upon earth in the last days. So I slept that night and another, like as he had commanded me.'[21] Esdras then had a 'dream' of a bizarre, three-headed, six-winged eagle, with 'hurtful claws', and of a roaring lion. 'And I saw and, behold, they appeared no more, and the whole body of the eagle was burnt, so that the earth was in great fear: then awaked I out of the trouble and trance of my mind and from great fear and said unto my spirit, Lo, this thou hast done unto me in that thou searchest out the ways of the

[20] 2 Esdras 10:26–38.
[21] 2 Esdras 10:52, 57–59.

47

Highest. Lo, yet am I weary in my mind and very weak in my spirit, and little strength is there in me, for the great fear wherewith I was affrighted this night . . . And he said unto me, This is the interpretation of the vision: The eagle, whom thou sawest come up from the sea, is the kingdom which was seen in the vision of thy brother Daniel . . . This is the dream that thou sawest and these are the interpretations. Thou only hast been meet to know this secret of the Highest. Therefore write all these things that thou hast seen in a book and hide them: and teach them to the wise of the people, whose hearts thou knowest may comprehend and keep these secrets. But wait thou here thyself yet seven days more that it may be shewed thee, whatsoever it pleaseth the Highest to declare unto thee. And with that he went his way.

'And it came to pass, when all the people saw that the seven days were past, and I not come again into the city, they gathered them all together, from the least unto the greatest, and came unto me and said, What have we offended thee ? and what evil have we done against thee that thou forsakest us and sittest here in this place.'[22]

Then he answered them, 'The Highest hath you in remembrance and the Mighty hath not forgotten you in temptation. As for me, I have not forsaken you, neither am I departed from you: but am come into this place to pray for the desolation of Sion, and that I might seek mercy for the low estate of your sanctuary. And now go your way home every man, and after these days will I come unto you . . . But I remained still in the field seven days as the angel commanded me and did eat only in those days of the flowers of the field, and had my meat of the herbs.'[23]

'And it came to pass after seven days, I dreamed a dream by night . . . And there came much people . . . whereof some were glad, some were sorry, some of them were bound, and other some brought of them that were offered: then was I sick through great fear.' Then the vision is interpreted and Esdras has a change of mood. 'Then went I forth into the field, giving praise

[22] 2 Esdras 12:3–5, 10–11, 35–41.
[23] 2 Esdras 12:47–49, 51.

and thanks greatly unto the most High because of his wonders, which he did in time.'[24]

'And it came to pass upon the third day, I sat under an oak and, behold, there came a voice out of a bush over against me, and said, Esdras, Esdras. And I said, Here am I, Lord. And I stood up upon my feet. Then he said unto me . . . for now hasteth the vision to come, which thou hast seen. Then answered I before thee and said . . . If I have found grace before thee, send the Holy Ghost into me and I shall write all that hath been done in the world from the beginning, which were written in thy law, that men may find thy path, and that they which live in the latter days may live. And he answered me, saying, Go thy way, gather the people together and say unto them, that they seek thee not for forty days. But look thou prepare thee many box trees [writing tablets], and take with thee Sarea, Dabria, Selemia, Ecanus, and Asiel, these five, which are ready to write swiftly; and come hither, and I shall light a candle of understanding in thine heart which shall not be put out, till the things be performed which thou shalt begin to write. And when thou hast done, some things shalt thou publish and some things shalt thou shew secretly to the wise: tomorrow this hour shalt thou begin to write. Then went I forth as he commanded and gathered all the people together and said . . . Let no man therefore come unto me now nor seek after me these forty days. So I took the five men as he commanded me, and went into the field and remained there. And the next day, behold, a voice called me, saying, Esdras, open thy mouth, and drink that I give thee to drink. Then I opened my mouth and behold, he reached me a full cup, which was full as it were with water, but the colour of it was like fire. And I took it and drank: and when I had drunk of it, my heart uttered understanding and wisdom grew in my breast, for my spirit strengthened my memory: and my mouth was opened and shut no more. The Highest gave understanding unto the five men, and they wrote the wonderful visions of the night that were told, which they knew not: and they sat forty days and they wrote in

[24] 2 Esdras 13:1, 13, 57.

the day and at night they ate bread. As for me, I spake in the day and I held not my tongue by night. In forty days they wrote two hundred and four books. And it came to pass, when the forty days were fulfilled, that the Highest spake, saying, The first that thou hast written publish openly, that the worthy and unworthy may read it: but keep the seventy last, that thou mayest deliver them only to such as be wise among the people: for in them is the spring of understanding, the fountain of wisdom, and the stream of knowledge. And I did so.'[25]

The drug coloured "like fire" evidently had an amphetamine-like action.

The rest of the book of Esdras seems to consist of the writings deemed fit to be read by both the worthy and the unworthy. The 'seventy last' were presumably put among the secret archives of the society of angels.

### Daniel's angel

Daniel is usually numbered among the prophets, but it is his association with the angel Gabriel that is of interest here.

The first six chapters of the Book of Daniel are clearly the work of popular hearsay and have that embellishment with the supernatural which so soon converts fact into preposterous myth. These chapters do not concern us here.

But the second six chapters are of a very different stuff. Daniel writes in the first person, and what he says is credible and fascinating.[26]

Daniel was a young captive in Babylon at the time when

[25] 2 Esdras 14:1–3, 18, 19, 22–27, 36–48.

[26] I am aware that it is established that the Book of Daniel, as we know it, was not written till 167 BC. Also that the last Babylonian king was one Nabonidus and that Belshazzar, his son, never was king. There must, however, have been some sort of regency during the madness of Nebuchadnezzar, and both Nabonidus and his son may have participated. But the quality of the circumstantial detail in the second half of the book of Daniel is such that whoever wrote it must have compiled it from earlier writings, probably Daniel's own.

'King Belshazzar' succeeded the mad King Nebuchadnezzar and he states that it was in the first year of Belshazzar's reign that he had his first experiences of 'dreams and visions upon his bed' in a manner that strikingly recalls the experiences of Esdras. In the visions there were the same bizarre horned beasts with eagles' wings, iron teeth and ten horns. Like Esdras, Daniel says, 'My spirit was grieved in the midst of my body and the visions of my head troubled me'.[27]

Daniel does not expressly say that an angel mentor was with him but he speaks of 'one of them that stood by' who interpreted the vision as Uriel had done for Esdras.

Later, in the third year of Belshazzar's reign, Daniel has another vision of rams, goats, horns and the heavenly host and it is clear that he is in a very confused and disorientated state. 'And it came to pass, when I, even I Daniel, had seen the vision, that I sought to understand it, and behold, there stood before me as the appearance of a man. And I heard a man's voice between the banks of Ulai, which called and said, Gabriel, make this man to understand the vision. So he came near where I stood; and when he came I was affrighted and fell upon my face: but he said unto me, Understand, O son of man, for the vision belongeth to the time of the end. Now as he was speaking with me, I fell into a deep sleep with my face toward the ground: but he touched me and set me upright.'[28] Gabriel duly interpreted the vision as Uriel had done for Esdras. 'And I Daniel fainted and was sick certain days: then I rose up and did the king's business; and I was astonished at the vision, but none understood it.'[29]

Later still, in the third year of Cyrus,[30] King of Persia, who had conquered Babylon, Daniel had another vision by the side of a river. 'In those days I, Daniel, was mourning three full

[27] Daniel 7:15.
[28] Daniel 8:15–18.
[29] Daniel 8:27.
[30] I have transposed the order of Chapters 9 and 10. The former begins, 'In the first year of Darius', and the latter, 'In the third year of Cyrus'. Cyrus was in fact earlier than Darius by some seventeen years.

weeks. I ate no pleasant bread, neither came flesh nor wine in my mouth, neither did I anoint myself at all, till three whole weeks were fulfilled. And in the four and twentieth day of the first month, as I was by the side of the great river which is Hiddekel, I lifted up mine eyes and looked and, behold, a man clothed in linen, whose loins were girded with pure gold of Uphaz: his body also was like the beryl, and his face as the appearance of lightning, and his eyes as lamps of fire, and his arms and his feet like in colour to burnished brass, and the voice of his words like the voice of a multitude. And I Daniel alone saw the vision: for the men that were with me saw not the vision, but a great quaking fell upon them, and they fled to hide themselves. So I was left alone and saw this great vision, and there remained no strength in me: for my comeliness was turned in me into corruption and I retained no strength. Yet heard I the voice of his words: and when I heard the voice of his words, then was I fallen into a deep sleep on my face, with my face toward the ground. And, behold, a hand touched me, which set me upon my knees and upon the palms of my hands. And he said unto me, O Daniel, thou man greatly beloved, understand the words that I speak unto thee, and stand upright: for unto thee am I now sent. And when he had spoken this word unto me, I stood trembling. Then said he unto me, Fear not, Daniel, for from the first day that thou didst set thine heart to understand and to humble thyself before thy God, thy words were heard, and I am come for thy words' sake. But the prince of the kingdom of Persia withstood me one and twenty days: but, lo, Michael, one of the chief princes, came to help me and I remained there with the kings of Persia. Now I am come to make thee understand what shall befall thy people in the latter days: for the vision is yet for many days. And when he had spoken unto me according to these words, I set my face toward the ground and was dumb. And, behold, one like the similitude of the sons of men touched my lips: then I opened my mouth, and spake, and said unto him that stood before me, O my Lord, by reason of the vision my sorrows are turned upon me and I retain no strength. For how can the servant of this my Lord talk with this my Lord? for as for me, straightway there remained no strength in me, neither was there breath left in me. Then there touched me again one like the appearance of a man and he strengthened me. And he said, O man greatly beloved, fear not: peace be unto thee, be strong, yea, be strong. And when he spake unto me, I was strengthened, and said, Let my lord speak, for thou hast strengthened me. Then said he, Knowest thou wherefore I am come unto thee? and now will I return to fight with the prince of Persia; and when I go forth lo, the prince of Greece shall come. But I will tell thee that which is inscribed in the writing of truth: and there is none that holdeth with me against these, but 'Michael your prince.'[31]

It is not clear whether the 'man clothed in linen' was an ordinary human angel transfigured in the eyes of Daniel by the hallucinogenic drug or whether he was wholly hallucination. We are told that the men who were with Daniel 'saw not the vision' but nevertheless ran away in fright. It may be that they recognized the linen-clad person as a holy man and were over-awed, as had been, much earlier, the men of Sodom. But it is quite clear that later in the session Daniel is in much physical distress and is tended and 'strengthened' by a human being.

It is interesting to note that the angel explains that he has been delayed for twenty-one days in Persia and has got away with the help of Michael, 'one of the chief princes'.

Daniel's last recorded interview with 'the man Gabriel' is much later, in the first year of Darius. There are no more visions. Daniel simply states what he has 'understood by the books' and says, 'And I set my face unto the Lord God, to seek by prayer and supplications, with fasting and sackcloth and ashes: and I prayed unto the Lord my God, and made my con-fession . . . Yea, whiles I was speaking in prayer, the man Gabriel, whom I had seen in the vision at the beginning, being caused to fly swiftly, touched me about the time of the evening oblation. And he instructed me and talked with me, and said, O Daniel, I am now come forth to make thee skilful of under-standing. At the beginning of thy supplications, the command-ment went forth and I am come to tell thee, for thou art greatly

[31] Daniel 10:2–21.

beloved: therefore consider the matter, and understand the vision.'[32] Gabriel then delivers a long speech of prophecy which may have been intelligible to Daniel but is not to us.[33] It could well have been dictated and taken down by Daniel.

At the end of the speech Gabriel adds, 'But thou, O Daniel, shut up the words and seal the book.'

This meeting with Gabriel seems to end in Daniel's seeing him off as he crosses a river. 'Then I Daniel looked and behold, there stood other two, the one on the brink of the river on this side, and the other on the brink of the river on that side. And one said to the man clothed in linen, which was above the waters of the river, How long shall it be to the end of these wonders? And I heard the man clothed in linen, which was above the waters of the river, when he held up his right hand and his left hand unto heaven, and sware by him that liveth for ever, that it shall be for a time, times, and an half; and when they have made an end of breaking in pieces the power of the holy people, all these things shall be finished. And I heard, but I understood not: then said I, O my Lord, what shall be the issue of these things? And he said, Go thy way, Daniel: for the words are shut up and sealed till the time of the end.'[34]

## Zechariah's angel

Zechariah was a young prophet in Babylon in the days of King Darius. To him the *word* of the Lord came, telling him to denounce the wickedness of the times and to foretell the appropriate doom. Most of his book consists of eloquence to this end but the first half-dozen chapters are an unmistakable account of a night spent beside the myrtle-trees beholding visions under the supervision of an unnamed angel—'the angel that talked

---

[32] Daniel 9:3, 4, 21–23.
[33] The prophecy begins at verse 24 of Chapter 9 and continues to verse 3 of Chapter 12, interrupted by the misplaced Chapter 10 which belongs to the earlier reign.
[34] Daniel 12:5–9.

with me'. A second angel that stood among the myrtle trees seems more likely to have been a part of the vision.

'I saw in the night and behold a man riding upon a red horse and he stood among the myrtle trees that were in the bottom: and behind him there were red horses, red, sorrel, and white. Then said I, O my Lord, what are these ? And the angel that talked with me said unto me, I will shew thee what these be. And the man that stood among the myrtle trees answered and said, These are they whom the Lord hath sent to walk to and fro through the earth . . . And the Lord answered the angel that talked with me with good words, even comfortable words. So the angel that talked with me said unto me, Cry thou, saying, Thus saith the Lord of hosts . . . And I lifted up mine eyes and saw, and behold four horns. And I said unto the angel that talked with me, What be these ? And he answered me, These are the horns which have scattered Judah, Israel, and Jerusalem . . . And I lifted up mine eyes and saw, and behold a man with a measuring line in his hand. Then said I, Whither goest thou ? And he said unto me, To measure Jerusalem, to see what is the breadth thereof and what is the length thereof. And, behold, the angel that talked with me went forth and another angel went out to meet him, and said unto him, Run, speak to this young man.'[35]

'And the angel that talked with me came again, and waked me, as a man that is wakened out of his sleep. And he said unto me, What seest thou ? And I said, I have seen and behold a candlestick all of gold, with its bowl upon the top of it, and its seven lamps thereon; there are seven pipes to each of the lamps, which are upon the top thereof: and two olive trees by it, one upon the right side of the bowl, and the other upon the left side thereof. And I answered and spake to the angel that talked with me, saying, What are these, my lord ? Then the angel that talked with me said unto me, Knowest thou not what these be ? And I said, No, my lord. Then he answered and spake unto me, saying, This is the word of the Lord unto Zerubbabel.'[36]

[35] Zechariah 1:8–10, 13, 14, 18, 19; 2:1–4.
[36] Zechariah 4:1–6.

'Then the angel that talked with me went forth . . . Then lifted I up mine eyes and saw, and behold, there came forth two women, and the wind was in their wings; now they had wings like the wings of a stork: and they lifted up the ephah between the earth and the heaven. Then said I to the angel that talked with me, Whither do these bear the ephah? And he said unto me, To build her an house in the land of Shinar; and when it is prepared she shall be set there in her own place.'[37]

'And again I lifted up mine eyes and saw, and behold, there came four chariots out from between two mountains . . . Then I answered and said unto the angel that talked with me, What are these, my lord? And the angel answered and said unto me, These are the four winds [or spirits] of heaven.'[38]

## Ezekiel's angel

Ezekiel was a priest and a captive in Babylon. Prophets and priests were usually hostile to one another, but Ezekiel became an eloquent preaching prophet, proclaiming whatever 'the word of the Lord' put into his mouth. His mandate as a prophet came to him in the fifth year of the captivity by the river Chebar where, he says, 'the heavens were opened and I saw visions of God'.

The visions that he describes are of the same bizarre 'living creatures', the same jewelled thrones and the same gorgeous colours as Esdras, Daniel and Zechariah beheld during their initiations, and may be attributed to the same medication, though he does not expressly state that it was an angel who administered it. But he does, after describing the glorious vision, say, 'And when I saw it, I fell upon my face and I heard a voice of one that spake. And he said unto me, Son of man, stand upon thy feet and I will speak with thee. And the spirit entered into me when he spake unto me and set me upon my feet and I heard him that spake unto me.'[39] It is probably fair

[37] Zechariah 5:5, 9-11.
[38] Zechariah 6:1, 4, 5.
[39] Ezekiel 1:28; 2:1, 2.

to assume that in this context the meaning of 'the spirit entered into me' is 'I regained full consciousness'.

He manages to stand upright and the human angel (if that is the nature of the 'one who spake') makes a short speech of ordination and then carries out a rite which still persists among the Muslim Kramu medicine-men of West Africa. These men copy out passages of the Koran and then crumble the written sheets into water for the patients or supplicants to drink. 'But thou, son of man, hear what I say unto thee; be not thou rebellious like that rebellious house; open thy mouth and eat that I give thee. And when I looked, behold, an hand was put forth unto me and, lo, a roll of a book was therein: and he spread it before me and it was written within and without: and there was written therein lamentations, and mourning, and woe. And he said unto me, Son of man, eat that thou findest; eat this roll, and go, speak unto the house of Israel. So I opened my mouth, and he caused me to eat the roll. And he said unto me, Son of man, cause thy belly to eat and fill thy bowels with this roll that I give thee. Then did I eat it and it was in my mouth as honey for sweetness.'[40]

Then follows a seven-day period of mental confusion and perhaps some dissociation, during which Ezekiel is recovering from the side-effects of the drug. These seem to include that buzzing in the ears which some drugs do produce. 'And I heard the noise of the wings of the living creatures as they touched one another, and the noise of the wheels beside them, even the noise of a great rushing. So the spirit lifted me up and took me away, and I went in bitterness, in the heat of my spirit, and the hand of the Lord was strong upon me. Then I came to them of the captivity at Tel-abib, that dwelt by the river Chebar and to where they dwelt; and I sat there astonied [dazed] among them seven days.'[41] Ezekiel has evidently had an overdose of the drug. One of the weaknesses of primitive herbalists is their slapdash manner with quantities.

Ezekiel apparently accepts his vocation and thereafter there

[40] Ezekiel 2:8–10; 3:1–3.
[41] Ezekiel 3:13–15.

is hardly anyone or anything that he does not denounce. He even prophesies against the mountains.[42] When elders come to 'inquire of the Lord', he replies, 'As I live, saith the Lord God, I will not be inquired of by you.'[43]

In the sixth year of the captivity, a year after his initiation, he has another session of visions, this time apparently indoors, but 'according to the vision that I saw in the plain'. This time presumably he is given a milder dose of the drug and though he is confused he does not describe being 'astonied' for seven days. But his muddle-headed description does several times mention a 'man clothed in linen, with a writer's inkhorn by his side'. (The inkhorn possibly contains the drug.) He gives very little description of the visions but reiterates that they were the same as those he saw by the river Chebar.

'This is the living creature that I saw under the God of Israel by the river Chebar and I knew that they were cherubim. Every one had four faces apiece and every one four wings; and the likeness of the hands of a man was under their wings. And as for the likeness of their faces, they were the faces which I saw by the river Chebar, their appearances and themselves: they went everyone straight forward.'[44]

Thereafter for many years—he usually records the year—Ezekiel hears 'the word of the Lord' in the manner which was commonplace among fasting prophets and duly denounces contemporary wickedness. The famous chapter concerning the dry bones which came to life seems to describe a straightforward allegorical dream concerning his ambition—which he did in fact realize—of inspiring the captives to plan a return to Jerusalem and to revive their national life.

But in the twenty-fifth year of the captivity, twenty years after his first Chebar visions, Ezekiel has a third session, his written description of which is necessarily confused, but which seems to include a supervising man who merges from time to time into the shining scenery of the vision. 'And he brought me thither and, behold, there was a man, whose appearance was like the appearance of brass, with a line of flax in his hand, and a measuring reed, and he stood in the gate. And the man said

---

[42] Ezekiel 6:2; 36:1.    [43] Ezekiel 20:1-3.    [44] Ezekiel 10:20-22.

unto me, Son of man, behold with thine eyes and hear with thine ears, and set thine heart upon all that I shall shew thee; for to the intent that I might shew them unto thee art thou brought hither: declare all that thou seest to the house of Israel.'[45]

'Afterward he brought me to the gate, even the gate that looketh toward the east: and behold, the glory of the God of Israel came from the way of the east: and his voice was like the sound of many waters: and the earth shined with his glory. And it was according to the appearance of the vision which I saw, even according to the vision that I saw when I came to destroy the city, and the visions were like the vision that I saw by the river Chebar, and I fell upon my face. And the glory of the Lord came into the house by the way of the gate whose prospect is toward the east. And the spirit took me up and brought me into the inner court and behold, the glory of the Lord filled the house. And I heard one speaking unto me out of the house, and a man stood by me.'[46]

## St John's angel

Although the Book of the Revelation of St John the Divine is attached to the New Testament, its manifest affinity is to the Babylonian–Assyrian–Persian cult of angels. I therefore deem it meet to examine it here.

In its opening sentence the book is described as the revelation 'sent and signified' by 'an angel' to the writer John.

St John, like the other initiates, writes in the first person and tells how he is in retreat on the Isle of Patmos 'for the word of God'. He achieves exactly the same state of being 'in the spirit' and we can hardly doubt that he is given the same drug that was given to the captives. There are the same hydra-headed beasts, candlesticks, measuring rods, temples, gorgeous but anguished women, coloured horses, precious stones, winged angels and the same host of shining people—predestined to immortality—'whose names are written in the book of life from the foundation of the world'.

[45] Ezekiel 40:3, 4.    [46] Ezekiel 43:1–6.

It must be admitted that without the captives' narratives it would be difficult to discern the presence of John's human angel mentor, for the boundaries between vision and reality are more blurred than in the captives' accounts.

John begins by saying that he heard 'a great voice' telling him to write what he saw and send it to the 'seven churches of Asia' which are matter-of-factly named. Presumably this voice is that of the human angel amplified by the onset of the effects of the drug. 'And I turned to see the voice that spake with me. And being turned I saw seven golden candlesticks.' Among the candlesticks is a highly transfigured man with a countenance 'as the sun shineth in his strength'. That this is the human angel beginning to merge into the bright visions we are led to suppose by the next event, which repeats the captives' experiences of complete prostration by the drug. 'I fell at his feet as one dead. And he laid his right hand upon me, saying, Fear not.' Then follows the familiar speech of interpretation by the mentor. 'The seven stars are the angels of the seven churches and the seven candlesticks are the seven churches.'[47]

The next two chapters are nothing to do with heavenly visions. John seems to be in clear consciousness, writing to the human angel's dictation seven very dull letters—admonitory and sometimes fault finding—to the 'seven angels in charge of the seven churches of Asia'. We know nothing of these angels, who were no doubt also human, and are not concerned with them here. Possibly John's mentor angel was an illiterate using him as a secretary.

In the next chapter the visions begin in earnest. 'After these things I saw, and behold, a door was opened in heaven . . . straightway I was in the spirit: and behold, there was a throne set in heaven.' Then follows a very long and gorgeous pageant of heavenly visions.

Half-way through the visions there seems to be an interval during which the attendant mortal angel delivers another discourse of interpretation. 'And the angel said unto me, Wherefore didst thou wonder? I will tell thee the mystery of the woman and of the beast that carried her which hath seven heads and ten horns . . .'

[47] Revelation 1:20.

Then John describes a second session of visions, with what seems another break for talk with the mortal angel. 'And he saith unto me, Write, blessed are they which are bidden to the marriage supper of the Lamb. And he saith unto me, These are true words of God. And I fell down before his feet to worship him. And he saith unto me, See thou do it not: I am a fellow-servant with thee and with thy brethren that hold the testimony of Jesus: worship God: for the testimony of Jesus is the spirit of prophecy.'[48] Then the visions are resumed.

When all the visions are over, the presence of the mortal angel is unmistakable. 'And I John am he that heard and saw these things. And when I heard and saw, I fell down to worship before the feet of the angel which showed me these things. And he saith unto me, See thou do it not: I am a fellow-servant with thee and with thy brethren the prophets and with them which keep the words of this book: worship God. And he saith unto me, Seal not up the words of the prophecy of this book, for the time is at hand.'[49]

Two items of angel initiation ritual seem to be suggested by this narrative. The first repeats that seen among Kramu medicine men and also described by Ezekiel.[50] John says, 'I took the little book out of the angel's hand and ate it up, and it was in my mouth sweet as honey,[51] and as soon as I had eaten it my belly was bitter.'

The second suggestion is pure speculation. It concerns the new ceremonial names (Gabriel, Raphael etc.) taken by members of the secret society. 'To him that overcometh, to him will I give of the hidden manna'—manna, it will be recalled, was known as angel's food—'and I will give him a white stone and upon the stone a new name written which no one knoweth but he that receiveth it.'[52] It is possible that each angel carried such a stone and that on his death it passed to his successor in the society.

[48] Revelation 19:9, 10.
[49] Revelation 22:8–10.
[50] Ezekiel 3:1–3.
[51] It may be that the hallucinogenic drug produced sensations of sweetness in the mouth. A berry known in West Africa as 'Elephant's sweet berry' has the effect of making all food taken for the next few hours seem oppressively sweet.
[52] Revelation 2:17.

*The Secret Medication*

That the Babylonian society of angels practised what colonial governments called 'native medicine' is clear from the behaviour of Tobit's angel. Such medicine is of two kinds: first, magical ritual such as giving the patient a page of the Koran to swallow or enticing his evil spirit to enter a hen; and second, herbalism. The latter is often very valuable. As everyone knows, some of our own most useful drugs—morphine, atropine, curare, rauwolfia, quinine, cocaine, digoxin and others— began their medical careers as medicine-men's herbs. But when a herb is of genuine value most medicine men will go to any lengths to keep it a secret. We do not know how many valuable drugs have been lost to pharmacology in this way.

The use of mescalin (an extract of the cactus *Anhalonium Lewinii*) to produce visions and insights for the refreshment of the soul has long been known to Mexican Indians, who take it reverently at small and infrequent religious meetings.[53] This cactus does not grow in the Old World. Mildly hallucinogenic alkaloids are found in plants growing in and around the Arabian Peninsula, but none able to produce the vivid visions of the biblical texts has so far been described.[54]

---

[53] A knowledge of this drug has been popularized by Aldous Huxley in *The Doors of Perception*. Some effects of smaller doses are described by D. H. Lawrence in *The Woman who Rode Away*.

[54] Since this book was written, John Allegro has suggested that the fungus *Amanita muscaria* played a prominent part in biblical 'revelation'. Muscarine is not, however, richly hallucinogenic. A good popular account of its action, based on standard works on forensic medicine, is to be found in Dorothy Sayers' novel, *The Documents in the Case*.

Since going to press both Mrs Eva Meyerowitz and Professor Fortes have drawn my attention to the *Soma* mushroom of the oriental Veda cult. In an article by Claude Lévi-Strauss 'Les Champignons dans la Culture', *L'Homme*, Vol. X, MCMLXX, Cashier I, suggestions are made as to the botanical identity of Soma.

# Part III

# THE OLD
# TESTAMENT
# PROPHETS

# 7 Relevant Mental Mechanisms

Among the many mental mechanisms which modern psychology has shown to operate—some every day, some only infrequently —within the human mind, there are two which have to be understood before we can understand the behaviour of the Hebrew prophets.

The first is the mental process called *dissociation* on which is dependent the world-wide and age-old phenomenon of 'spirit possession'.

The second is *hallucination* (an extreme variant of the universal mental mechanism of *projection*) on which is dependent the experience of 'supernatural' visions and voices.

## SPIRIT POSSESSION

The phenomenon of 'spirit possession', often called 'trance' or 'oracular frenzy', has been known in its various modifications throughout the world from the beginning of history. It persists today wherever people are allowed to behave naturally, though it is not common in Europe. In Africa it has always flourished abundantly and today (as I shall recount later), far from dying out, it is experiencing a renaissance. Even in Britain, some entirely new manifestations have lately appeared.

### *The mental mechanism of dissociation*

'Spirit possession' is a perfectly natural phenomenon depending on the mental mechanism known to psychology as *dissociation*.

Ever since Pierre Janet described dissociation in his classic

*The Major Symptoms of Hysteria* (New York, 1907), psychiatrists, who have seen it only in patients, have assumed that it is *always* hysterically[1] occasioned. I do not believe this. Laughter and tears, which are equally weird phenomena and certainly *can* be hysterical, can also be a profoundly therapeutic release of tension.

An outline of the observable behaviour of the dissociated mind must first be given.

In the dissociated state the everyday 'stream of consciousness' is split into parallel streams,[2] one of which possesses the entire field of awareness, the rest being temporarily obliterated. We are all familiar in some degree with separated parallel streams of mental activity. A skilled musician can read new music at the piano and think about his overdraft at the same time. A clever arithmetician can add up three columns of figures simultaneously while discussing the lawn-mower with his wife: he is operating two major streams and three sub-streams. Anyone who drives a car knows that one part of his mind looks after the driving 'automatically' while the rest ranges freely. But in this everyday experience the separated streams can be brought instantly back into one at the demand of the moment. In the dissociated state of mind the familiar stream of awareness goes into abeyance—into sleep, if you will—and a split-off

---

[1] Hysteria has never been satisfactorily defined. It is usually assumed to be always motivated by a desire to gain cheaply a position which enables the patient to shirk his burdens and responsibilities, as in 'conversion hysteria', where he puts himself out of the fray by developing, say, a paralysed limb.

[2] This is of course a simplified spatial metaphor, conveniently summing up the observed facts. Very complex processes of selection and segregation must be at work in the mind. Laymen should note that this splitting of the stream of consciousness is nothing to do with schizophrenia. Psychiatrists also should note that the unconscious part of the mind in dissociated states has nothing to do with the Freudian 'unconscious.' The latter is a theorist's creation, the former is an observable phenomenon. *Vide* Bernard Hart, *The Conception of Dissociation*, British Journal of Medical Psychology, vol. VI, part 4, 1926.

stream takes control. When the person comes out of this dissociated state he does not remember what the split-off part of
his mind did, or made him do, under the eyes of his neighbours,
during the episode. This happens also in sleep-walking and, to
a very small extent, in all ordinary sleep, as anyone may prove
by gently pulling away the blankets from a sleeper: he will
intelligently pull them back without waking. Many children
can get up at night and relieve their bladders without waking.
When a mother sleeps through a deafening thunderstorm but
wakes at the smallest squeak of her baby, she is aroused by a
specially mandated split-off part of her mind which has remained awake. Anyone who decides, when he goes to bed, that
he will wake at some appointed early hour usually does so; he
has successfully commanded a split-off fragment of his mind to
stay awake and call him.

In the classic case-books of psychiatry there are variants and
elaborations of the dissociation mechanism, which need not
concern us here.[3] The phenomenon, as I have observed it during
thirty-five years in some thousands of cases of 'spirit possession',
is as straightforward as normal sleep, and I do not believe it to
be—in its African context—any more pathological than sleep.
It conforms to a constant pattern as follows.

*The observable phenomena of 'spirit possession'*

The occasion of possession is most often a festival dance or other
religious gathering with drumming and exciting music. The
person is sitting quietly, looking or listening, or he may be
casually dancing. If sitting, he begins to look dazed and
oppressed and when addressed is inaccessible and mute. If he is
dancing, he slows down and hesitates. This inconspicuous dazed
phase lasts only a few minutes and then, very suddenly, gives

[3] Examples of Jekyll-and-Hyde separations of incompatible
character traits, 'loss of memory' with sudden restoration and
amnesia for the interval, and automatic writing are among the
well-documented rarer variants of dissociation. Hypnosis is a
commoner variant.

way to the dramatic excited phase which lasts an hour or several hours. The person springs into activity—dancing, quivering, leaping, often performing unwonted feats of strength and endurance. 'Something has come to him.'[4] If he is an unconditioned novice, 'strongly' possessed, he may, unless restrained, rush blindly off into the bush, so fleetly and so far that he may get lost and perish of thirst and starvation. Sometimes he remains alive in the bush for weeks, eating from banana farms, and then comes home. Sometimes he stays there so long that he becomes demented and does not want to return. I know an old man whose twin brother was 'taken' in this way to bush and stayed there for years, occasionally seen by hunters and farmers, naked, with his hair grown long, resisting all attempts to bring him home. When no-one had seen him for years it was assumed that he was dead.

The untrained novice is usually mute during possession though he often produces *glossolalia*—the babbling of meaningless syllables of baby-talk and gibberish. But after a number of episodes, disciplined by expert training, he becomes able to sing, shout, speak and finally answer questions and make speeches. He is then believed to be the mouthpiece of unseen powers and his oracular utterances are treasured.

The face of a possessed person usually bears an abstracted dreamy look or may be mask-like. He does not appear to feel pain, fatigue or thirst, though he will automatically and greedily swallow a long drink if it is held to his lips. In some parts of the world, possessed persons cut themselves with knives (as did the priests of Baal[5]), walk on red-hot cinders, gouge out their eyeballs and inflict on themselves various other physical outrages without apparent pain. The reader may recall the accounts of the priests of Cybele under the Emperor Claudius. 'Clad in black robes, her "fanatics" as they were called, would turn round and round to the sound of drums and trumpets, with their long loose hair streaming and when vertigo seized them

---

[4] 'Something has come to him' is the reverse of the truth. Something has, in fact, gone from him.

[5] 1 Kings 18:28.

and a state of anaesthesia was attained, they would strike their arms and bodies great blows with swords and axes . . . Finally a prophetic delirium would overcome them and they foretold the future . . . Mingling their piercing cries with the shrill sound of flutes, the Galli [Cybele's priests] flagellated themselves and cut their flesh, and neophytes performed the supreme sacrifice [castration] with the aid of a sharp stone, being insensible to pain in their frenzy.'[6]

But in West Africa there are no such monstrous practices. There, as everywhere else, words and actions in the dissociated state are simply an uninhibited expression of those thoughts and feelings which are the main preoccupation of conscious life.

The spectacular physical feats which some possessed people are able to perform are probably to be explained by the temporary loss of that self-observation and self-solicitude which restrain the rest of us—except perhaps the most highly trained and dedicated athletes—from expending our physical energy down to its ultimate reserves. Most of us, when we become short of breath, decide that we have done all we can: the athlete knows that he can run up an 'oxygen debt' which enables him for a time to live in excess of his oxygen income: the shaman does not observe his own breathlessness and fatigue.

I have seen grossly fat old women, who normally could hardly waddle about, whirl nimbly round the dance arena, leaping high into the air. The strongly possessed novice, with the urge to rush away into the bush, requires the united strength of all the most muscular young men of the village to restrain him and, if he does escape them, his turn of speed ensures that he will not be caught till the spirit has left him. Some good witnesses told me of several untrained novices who were violently possessed for such long stretches—more than a day as against the normal hour or two—that they died of exhaustion. As might be expected, people with defective hearts or coronary impairment sometimes die on the dance floor. This is taken to be the result of envious bad magic by rivals, and most shamans are careful to equip themselves with protective

---

[6] Franz Cumont, *The Oriental Religions in Roman Paganism* (authorized translation), Chicago, 1911.

counter-magics. The most remarkable example of super-normal physical achievement was given me by many good witnesses who had seen the last days of a dearly loved old priest who was dying of pulmonary tuberculosis. Though weak and gasping, he would nevertheless rise from his bed and be shaken by great gales of furious dancing and oracular utterance.

The end of the excitement is abrupt. The person usually flings himself into the arms of friends, collapses limply and then immediately becomes normal. His abstracted expression gives way dramatically to one of appropriate fatigue and bodily discomfort as he becomes aware of his aching limbs, thirst and so on. If he has spent his energy down to the utmost dregs he may sink into exhausted sleep then and there, but usually he walks home, takes a bath and food, and sleeps normally. He describes a complete amnesia for everything he did or said during the 'possessed' period. To this important point we shall return later.

Another important point is that possession is followed by an aftermath of peaceful euphoria. This, of course, may be masked by extreme exhaustion and physical discomfort, but a person who is possessed temperately and often may feel his whole life to be pervaded by a sustaining contentment. We shall return to this very important aspect of spirit possession.


## The Induction of Possession

The state of 'possession' can be occasioned in various ways. One of these is fasting. Many a man's first episode of possession occurs when, having gone out in the morning to his farm or to hunt without his breakfast, he is delayed by some chance and fasts till evening: he is then seen to 'come home shaking because something has come to him'.

The commonest occasion of a first 'possession' and of all subsequent 'possessions' is the exciting rhythmic drumming, gong-gong beating and other music of a dance. Many ordinary people become mildly possessed at dances and the next day quietly resume their normal routine.

Another potent precipitant of dissociation is sudden strong emotion—fear, grief, joy, anger, religious awe and wonder, indignation, or any scene of great public excitement. To see a person or a tree struck by lightning or to see a fireball in a thunderstorm may send a witness into dissociation. At a funeral the pall-bearers may become possessed, and so may the bearers of sacred insignia in processions. There are stories told of days of warfare when every warrior took to the campaign a small retinue of camp followers to carry his provisions and to accompany him into the firing-line for the reloading of his guns. Often these battle attendants included women and girls and sometimes, when a man was killed, his wife or daughter, smitten with grief and anger, would become possessed and rush wildly into the enemy's lines, terrifying the troops not only by the horrible fury of her onslaught but by the belief that supernatural powers were in action. In the nineteen-thirties I attended the funerals of several old women who were given full military honours because of the parts they had played in such scenes. Again, in the old days of lagoon worship it was the custom to make an annual sacrifice of a young virgin by drowning her in the lagoon. Usually she became possessed and leapt joyfully into the water without compulsion. This entitles us to speculate concerning the state of mind of the martyrs who went singing into the arena or to the stake. In the religious meetings of some of the new Christian cults in Ghana, not only do many of the congregation become possessed—as they believe—by the Holy Ghost, in the tumult of the drumming and singing, but a greater number succumb in the quieter but more emotional moment of being anointed with oil. The anointed worshipper sways on his knees, falls over unconscious, and is carried out. I do not think this is ordinary fainting. I think the dissociation process aborts in the first phase, as I have sometimes, but less often, seen it do in the ancient traditional assemblies.

When a private consultant diviner wishes to go into the possessed state to answer a client's questions, he often gazes into a black bowl of liquid to the accompaniment of monotonously clanging gong-gongs.

There are occasions when dissociation is induced for therapeutic purposes. When it is desired to drive out of a person a tiresome spirit of ill-luck which is for ever bringing him mishap, he is made to hold on his head a heavy weight, a bowl of medicine or a live fowl, while the physician and his assistants sing, clap and beat their iron gong-gongs. The patient responds first by becoming dazed and then suddenly he dashes off into the bush where, it is hoped, he leaves the troublesome spirit for good. At any rate the post-possessional euphoria makes him *feel* that he has so left it.

Psychiatric hypnotists know that small sub-toxic doses of ether or nitrous oxide will sometimes help to induce the hypnotic state. Similarly, the Dagomba of Ghana induce dissociation in their priests and priestesses by causing them to inhale the fumes produced by throwing into a charcoal fire a herbal powder whose composition they keep secret. This was the method of the Delphic Sibyls who inhaled, according to some authorities, the fumes of a poisonous mushroom and, it is recorded by some of their contemporaries,[7] all died young. Though priests in West Africa are forbidden to take alcohol on their days of worship, laymen sometimes complain that very small doses of alcohol—insufficient to cause drunkenness— throw them into a state of possession which makes them take to their heels and run for miles. The dissociating dose is smaller than the intoxicating dose.

Another aid to dissociation is 'conditioning'. Just as most of us are conditioned to fall asleep in an accustomed place at an accustomed time, so the habituated shaman usually responds quickly on the right occasion. A priest whom I knew in Ashanti took influenza during an epidemic: after it, feeling weak and washed out, he wanted to avoid being possessed, so he was careful to keep out of his god's sanctuary, where, he said, the spirit would come on him at once.

Another factor which can affect the onset of dissociation is contagion. We all know that laughter, yawning and various other natural phenomena are contagious. So, too, in an assembly,

---

[7] Lucan, *Pharsalia*, translated by Robert Graves, Penguin 1956.

possession may hang fire, but the first person to succumb will trigger off the others.

Some habituated diviners can throw themselves into dissociation at will, in much the same way as a few enviable people among ourselves can take a nap anywhere and at any time.

The resemblance between dissociation and sleep appears again. In everyday conditions—aside from the grossest fatigue —no one need fall asleep if determined against it. Similarly, the dissociation impulse can be resisted. Dissociation is rare among those literate Africans who despise the old heathen ways, but (as we shall see later) in the new 'spiritual' Christian cults it is welcomed and fully practised.

*Termination of the dissociated state*

Habit and convenience usually dictate how long a person shall remain possessed, just as our own waking from sleep is so ordained. Possessed people at a festival dance come out of their trances when the guests are ready to go home or when they themselves must think about catching the passenger-lorry.

When a possessed priest is answering the questions of supplicants, a silly question or the confession of some shocking sin may exasperate or anger the possessing deity and he will suddenly desert his medium. One may suspect that this also happens when the deity is nonplussed by a question. I recall an occasion when a woman supplicant complained of a recurring impulse to kill her children with a cutlass. This type of impulse is common among obsessive-compulsive patients in Europe, but such personalities are rare in West Africa. Depressed and self-denigrating witches believe themselves capable of spreading an intangible destructive *influence* but not of employing weapons and other concrete agents. This supplicant's complaint was therefore outside the diviner's experience: he was so much startled and shocked that the spirit fled from him immediately.

## Loss of the ability to dissociate

Most people experience an occasional sleepless night. So too the habituated priest or priestly auxiliary may have an occasional day when the spirit capriciously fails to come. If he is an avaricious diviner for money, he may 'put on an act' and deceive the supplicant, but most priests are afraid of displeasing their deities and do not cheat.

Just as a distressing spell of insomnia may afflict anyone who is in anxiety, so too guilt and worry may send a shaman to a neighbouring shaman complaining that the spirit has deserted him. Often the anxiety is caused by neglect of the possessing deity's ordinances. For instance, priests are enjoined to fast and take no alcohol on their days of worship and to avoid sleeping with their wives on the eve of such a day. We shall return later to this matter of the inhibition of dissociation.

## The making of a shaman

When a person is possessed for the first time at a dance or other excited gathering, no one takes much notice so long as he stays in the dance and does nothing extravagant. He probably comes back to normal, goes quietly home, and is not possessed again till the next dance. If however he is violently possessed, rushes blindly away into the bush and has to be brought back by search parties, or if when he gets home he begins to be possessed several times a week, then it is decided that he is marked out for a dedicated career. A deity 'wants to come to him and work'. He is then sent to an established priest or private consultant diviner for training. There his behaviour gradually becomes controlled and conditioned according to the accepted ceremonial routine, and he no longer charges off into the bush to his own peril. Gradually he learns to talk while possessed, tells his trainers the name of his possessing deity and is finally a fluent oracle, replying to supplicants' questions. Most priests are possessed only by one deity, but some priestly auxiliaries, private soothsayers and medicine-men's auxiliaries have extensive repertoires. Any one of these more versatile shamans may be possessed at a dance by a succession of spirits—a dead and gone warrior shouting war songs and brandishing a sword, a gracious old ancestress beaming on her posterity, an animal-god going on all fours, biting, snarling, catching fowls and eating pieces of them alive. Psychologically these 'personalities' are all artefacts created by complex mental mechanisms out of traditional ideas.

Shamanism is not the resort of hysterical maladjusted personalities. During the training of a priest or diviner he submits to a good deal of self-discipline. He practises chastity, drinks no alcohol, fasts on his holy days (usually three in a week), and does a good deal of menial work for his trainer. Once he is established on his own, his success in his profession depends more on those qualities which bring success in any other profession than on any startling oracular utterances.

Students of Ashanti history know that when the Ashanti Confederacy was formed for the purpose of rebelling against the galling yoke of the Denchera overlord, the brain that conceived that organization, and the energy and skill that built it up, belonged to a shaman (*komfo*) called Komfo Anoche. His authority as the mouthpiece of a divine power was what first assured him of a hearing and lent weight to his dicta, but his own endowment of high intelligence, courage and leadership carried the enterprise through.

*Oracular utterances*

Most oracular utterances—with the exception of novices' gibberish (glossolalia)—are commonplace pieces of sensible advice, which the supplicant's neighbours may have given him fruitlessly many times. But endowed with the divine authority of the deity they are accepted without demur. Often the oracle reproves the supplicant for some peccadillo—say an illicit love affair—which everyone knows of, but has not openly mentioned. Traditional morality can always be certain of oracular support.

When oracular utterance startles it is usually by reason of its daring. It is no respecter of persons and no one, however exalted his position, is immune from its criticism or reproof. The possessed shaman is exonerated from personal responsibility for his utterances. They are not his but those of his possessing spirit. He does not even know, when the spirit has left him, what it said when it was upon him. I was told of an occasion when an obscure little rural priest travelled a hundred miles to administer a rebuke to the King of Ashanti. He arrived at the palace door in a state of possession. The king was told; he dropped all other business and admitted the visitor into his presence. There the possessing deity proclaimed some unpalatable truths. No *personal* impertinence was imputed to the priest. He was treated with the most respectful courtesy. Very different was my own reception by the same King of Ashanti when, endowed only with the mundane authority of Britain's Medical Research Council, I wrote asking for a little cooperation which would have been of great help to my work. I received only a curt snub.

It must be stressed that nothing comes out of a possessed shaman's mind that has not been put into it by normal processes. We must now consider some of the *apparent* contradictions to this statement.

Firstly, oracular utterances sometimes achieve a wisdom exceeding that of the shaman's normal capacity. It may well be that the dissociated mind, shuttered off from the distractions of normal consciousness, can concentrate on relevant facts, marshal them and draw conclusions from them more swiftly and ably than at other times. There is a close resemblance between dissociation, sleep and hypnosis: it is a common experience to solve a troublesome problem in one's sleep: it is also true that in hypnosis people are capable of surprising feats of memory.

Secondly, in West Africa possessed persons are often able to speak languages which they cannot normally speak. However, it is always found, on investigating their life histories, that at some period in childhood they were exposed to the languages in question and subsequently forgot them. It may well be that the dissociated mind has access to recesses of memory which are closed to normal consciousness.

A third claim sometimes made for the dissociated mind is that of paranormal cognition. This, if true, is again partly explicable by the resemblance between dissociation and sleep. It has been established by sober investigators that dreams occasionally rehearse future events and spatially remote events.[8] More recent work has established the scientific respectability of the notion of extra-sensory perception and it may well be that, in the dissociated state, the mind, being for the time screened from the normal inflow of sensory stimuli, is more receptive of those extra-sensory stimuli of whose nature we are as yet ignorant.[9]

Among the social uses of possession are the peculiar benefits it offers to ordinary people in distress. When such a supplicant comes to the shrine of a deity or to a private consultant diviner, he usually comes in anxiety and indecision about alternative lines of conduct. To the possessing deity he is made to confess his sins, which in itself lifts a weight from his mind, and he is given a commonsense line of conduct to follow: he can follow it without loss of face for it is divinely prescribed. If he comes in fear, as many do, feeling that envious rivals are out to destroy him, he is promised the deity's protection, and if he complains of being dogged by misfortune he is promised divine aid. The impressive spectacle of the priest, divested of his normal personality and endowed with a supposedly divine one is matchless in its reassurance and the supplicant goes home soothed, consoled and strengthened.

[8] J. W. Dunne, *An Experiment with Time,* London, 1927. Of this A. S. Eddington wrote, ' My own feeling is that the "becoming" is really there in the physical world but is not formulated in the description of it in classical physics.'

[9] L. J. Bendit, *Paranormal Cognition,* London, 1944 (this was accepted by Cambridge University as an M.D. thesis); J. B. Rhine, *New Frontiers of the Mind,* London, 1950.

*Consultation and supplication procedures*

When a priest or other shaman is in the state of 'possession' by his deity, that deity, being present with him, is available to be either implored or consulted. There are various procedures, most of which do not concern us here, but the commonest is that known in Ashanti as *abisa* (inquiry). The possessed priest stands just outside the door of his sanctuary, facing the standing congregation. One by one the supplicants come forward and lay before him their problems or their requests. The deity gives either a solution or a promise of help. As we shall note later, an identical procedure is described in the Old Testament.

## VISIONS AND VOICES

People who hear supernatural voices or see fairies and other things which no one else can see are hallucinated: they have false sense impressions which do not correspond with external fact. These impressions come from within themselves but, by the mental mechanism known as *projection*, seem to come from without.

Hallucination is an extreme variant, a specialized case, of the process of projection. Projection in its less florid forms is known to all of us, so must be examined before focusing on hallucination.

Projection is the detachment or dislocation from the mind's system of ideas of some fragment or tangled knot of fragments and the attachment of this to some external person, real or imagined. The motive of this mental action is usually the avoidance of the discomfort of difficult or unpalatable mental reorganization. A very clear example happened to me: I dreamt that a patient had cramp in the foot and was squirming in pain while I massaged the foot. I woke up to find that the cramp was in my own foot. I had *projected* my own disorder on to an imaginary outsider, my motive being to preserve my own comfortable state of sleep.

Everyday life, as well as dream life, is full of self-deceiving projections, some commonplace, harmless and helpful, others blatant and pernicious. Many lonely children create imaginary playmates with all their own hopes and fears, and commune happily with these wholly understanding *confidantes*. Adult projections are easier to perceive in others than in ourselves: we all notoriously condemn in others the faults that lurk in ourselves, that is, we project our own defects into a place where they can comfortably be denounced. The nation that complains that other nations are encircling it is usually harbouring similar ambitions of its own. The drunkard who complains that his wife's mismanagement has broken up the home is unwilling to contemplate the effects of his own behaviour.

Mental hospitals are full of the grosser manifestations of this phenomenon. The patient who complains that the neighbours are plotting to seduce his wife is usually concealing lecherous urges of his own. The elderly daughter who has for many years nursed a very aged and querulous mother imagines that she hears wicked neighbours saying, 'That old woman ought to be put down.'

Religion is full of projections. Everyone who worships a god projects his own image in some measure upon that god. The man who looks around the world and is filled only with compassion is the one who (if he be a mystic[10]) will feel himself to be enveloped and irradiated by the love of God. The strong but overtaxed leader whose nature is to be leant upon by others is the man whose god will say to him, 'My presence shall go with thee and I will give thee rest.' Gods can also be the receptacles of the basest impulses. Every nation that goes to war persuades itself that its god commands this. The most repulsive acts of violence committed by the immigrating Israelites on the

---

[10] William James, in his great classic, *The Varieties of Religious Experience*, simply reports what people have said about their subjective experiences. He has nothing there to say of mental mechanisms. James's book should be read by all who vaguely imagine that mysticism means magic, astrology and the rope trick. Evelyn Underhill's classic *Mysticism*, and Aldous Huxley's *The Perennial Philosophy* will also be of service.

innocent inhabitants of the promised land were perpetrated in the conviction that Jehovah had ordained this.

In considering hallucination—that specially commanding type of projection which invades the realm of sense impressions—we have two questions to ask. Firstly, what determines the hallucinated *state* of mind ? Secondly, what determines the *content* of the hallucination ?

As to the first, probably the determinant is ultimately always chemical. Everyone knows that there are hallucinogenic drugs and that there are illnesses which produce hallucinogenic toxins. The disease schizophrenia,[11] in which hallucination is very common, is believed by many authorities to be determined by a defect in adrenalin metabolism.[12] Again, prolonged fasting brings chemical changes in the blood which have long been known to favour hallucination. An old Ashanti said, 'You cannot hear the voice of your god when you are full of food.'

In most biblical hallucinations the favourable conditions were probably hunger and thirst. Very few people in our own society have ever been hungry for more than a few hours, but to the writer of Revelation a place where 'they shall hunger no more, neither shall they thirst any more' was his idea of Heaven. Isaiah, seeking an example of disillusionment, writes of what was no doubt a common wish-fulfilment dream, 'And it shall be as when a hungry man dreameth and, behold, he eateth; but he awaketh and his soul is empty: or as when a thirsty man dreameth and, behold, he drinketh; but he awaketh and, behold, he is faint.'[13]

Again, it may be that there are a few people (perhaps there

---

[11] Schizophrenia does *not* mean '*split mind*' in the sense popularly supposed. It is a grave disease sometimes leading to complete mental disintegration.

[12] In West Africa when a person is in a prolonged state of extreme terror his distraction often changes after a few days to a much quieter state indistinguishable from classic schizophrenia. It may be supposed that the excessive outpouring of adrenalin caused by the fear is at the bottom of this phenomenon. When the cause of the fear is removed the patient quickly becomes normal.

[13] Isaiah 29:8.

were some among the ancient Hebrews) who have unusual processes of metabolism which produce hallucinogenic chemicals. The uncommon metabolic process called alkaptonuria produces not hallucination but black urine and has no other observable effect.

As to the *content* of the hallucination, that is where the projection comes in. The hallucinatory voices may reproach, threaten, reassure or command, depending on the person's anxieties, ambitions, loves, hates, fears, humiliations, frustrations, secret desires, and so on. In most toxic hallucinations there is no important content at all but only the trivial surface small-talk of the mind, as when we look out of a train window and say to ourselves, 'What a good apple orchard' or 'What a lot of cows.' A hallucinated patient told me that when she heard footsteps in the corridor a voice said, 'Footstep, footstep, footstep', and that when people came into the room a voice announced their names. A medical officer told me that once when he had malaria on a long and tedious train journey and was heavily dosed with quinine, he began to hear a band playing in the guard's van, and it was only when he found that this band would change its tune to whatever he silently commanded it that he realized the music was hallucinatory.

Because most of our knowledge of hallucination and projection has come to us from mental hospitals, we are prone to think of these processes as always pathological. But there are occasions, often of desperate emergency, when the subject's most admirable qualities are projected in a manner which enables him to extricate himself from dire straits. For instance, I knew of an English farm labourer who was attacked by a bull and flung to the ground. Then he heard a commanding voice say loudly and clearly, 'Get your finger into his nose ring.' He obeyed and was able to control the bull and save his own life. No doubt his own knowledge and resourcefulness condensed themselves into this helpful projection while the metabolites of adrenalin provided the chemical basis. Again, I read of a merchant seaman who fell overboard unnoticed by any shipmates. He swam for some time and when about to give up in despair he heard the voice of his little daughter calling out, 'Keep on swimming,

Daddy.' This galvanized him into further effort: he had the good luck to be picked up by another ship and lived to tell the tale. Here we have a man's own qualities of courage and parental love projecting themselves into an inspiriting voice.

There are emergencies when the mental process stops just short of producing clear hallucination, and produces the sense of a presence. But this sense, it seems, carries all the conviction of a sense impression. In *Camp Six*, F. S. Smythe's account of the unsuccessful 1933 attempt on Everest, the writer describes such an experience. He is on the way down the mountain alone and it is doubtful whether he can reach safety. He writes, 'After leaving Eric a strange feeling possessed me that I was accompanied by another . . . This "presence" was strong and friendly. In its company I could not feel lonely, neither could I come to any harm. It was always there to sustain me on my solitary climb up the snow-covered slabs. Now, as I halted and extracted some mint cake from my pocket, it was so near and so strong that instinctively I divided the mint into two halves and turned round with one half in my hand to offer it to my companion.'[14] Here we have the mountaineer's qualities of courage, self-reliance and friendliness condensing into the near-embodiment of an external helper.

Again, years ago I was staying in a remote African village where one of my friends was the priest of Sakumo, the pagan deity of the local lagoon. The village was in a state of political turmoil which had destroyed many people's happiness and threatened to break up the ancient traditions. This was a deep grief to the priest, who was a gentle and godly man, full of love for his ancient calling. Someone had asked him to curse the malefactors to his god but he replied in bewilderment, 'I don't know how to curse, I only know how to bless.' One night, he told me, when all the village was asleep, he went to the grove of his god, to pour his weekly libations and pray for the welfare of the village. This done, he sat in the dark grove in a state of deep dejection brooding on the sorrows of the village. Then, he told me, the god Sakumo came into the grove and stood beside him.

14 F. S. Smythe, *Camp Six*, London, 1937.

He did not see or hear him but was strongly aware of his presence. The god spoke to him, though not in audible words, saying, 'Don't worry. I know all about your troubles. I am looking after you.' The god stayed a little while in the grove, standing beside the seated priest. Then he went away. The priest remained sitting for some time, with a wonderful sense of peace and joy flooding his being. The next day, he said, he felt so happy that he went to his farm and worked harder than he had ever worked in his life.

As I see this incident, the simple-minded old man's love and compassion for the people of his village and his desire to comfort them were projected into a presence which brought peace and comfort to himself.

Most biblical hallucinations cannot be regarded as either pathological or important. When the voice of God came to a prophet telling him to rise and cry against some evil-doer, it was only telling him to do what he would probably have done in any case, but it gave him the confidence to do it publicly and with passion. As we have seen, other 'men of God' called angels who, as far as we know, heard no commanding voices and were driven by no other supposedly supernatural force, went quietly to evil-doers and rebuked them in the same terms as did the hallucinated prophets, but with less sound and fury.

# 8 The Prophets One by One

*Introduction*

The word prophet (Greek *prophetes*) means 'one who speaks for another, especially one who speaks for a god and interprets his will to man'.[1]

The Hebrew prophets of the Old Testament appear to have been of three kinds.

Firstly, there were those who simply had dreams: 'The prophet that hath a dream, let him tell a dream; and he that hath my word, let him speak my word faithfully.'[2]

Secondly, there were those to whom 'the word' of the Lord came. These were auditorily hallucinated. 'The Lord spake with Moses . . . and the Lord spake unto Moses face to face as a man speaketh unto his friend.'[3]

Thirdly, there were the most interesting prophets of all, those who were intermittently possessed by 'the spirit of the Lord', in the manner still observable in West Africa.

The Hebrew word translated 'spirit' is *ruach* and means a wind or moving air. The Greek word is *pneuma*, meaning air or breath. The Ashanti word is *honhom*, linked with *home*, to breathe.

The biblical descriptions of seizure by the spirit are variously worded, but always the prophet is suddenly excited and physically moved by it as a passive agent. Some were moved 'mightily' and performed feats of strength. Of others we are told that the spirit 'came upon him', 'entered into him', 'filled him', 'fell upon him', 'moved him', 'set him on his feet',

---

[1] Liddell and Scott, *Greek/English Lexicon*, Oxford.

[2] Jeremiah 23:28.

[3] Exodus 33:9, 11.

'lifted him up'. Of anyone who was made to rush away into the bush it was said that the spirit 'took him', 'drove him', 'carried him', or 'caught him away'. Of others it was said that the spirit 'rested upon them'. This expression is used in Ashanti[4] and can also be translated 'descend upon' or 'perch upon'—in the manner of a bird. Sometimes of a possessed prophet it was said that 'the hand of the Lord' was upon him.

Some prophets were also priests. At least three seem to have held the official post of rain-maker. But most of them were stern critics of the establishment and fearlessly denounced all unrighteousness, no matter whose. They did this with impunity so long as the personage denounced was in fealty to the same god as was the prophet. 'Then said the princes and all the people unto the priests and to the prophets, This man is not worthy of death, for he hath spoken to us in the name of the Lord our God.'[5] But a king worshipping Baal was not afraid to slay a prophet of Jehovah. Zechariah, the son of Jehoida, was stoned by princes who served 'groves and idols'. The prophet Urijah was slain by King Jehoiakim, but we gather that Jehoiakim had deserted the worship of Jehovah. Also, it seems, a prophet could curse or bless only the worshippers of his own god. Thus when Balak, king of Moab, needed the services of a prophet to curse the Israelites, he had to find a prophet of the Israelites' own god to do this.

Some prophets were also consultant diviners or seers, supplying, for a fee, the answers to supplicants' questions. They may have supplemented the prophetic method by devices akin to the Urim and Thummim, by breaking eggs, by examining the entrails of slaughtered fowls, or by the stars.

Most prophets gave only such advice as any intelligent contemporary could have given. Elisha evidently knew something of irrigation. Elijah revived the widow's son with the 'kiss of life'. Isaiah, who cured King Hezekiah's boil with a poultice of figs, knew about osmosis. The prophets of doom who foretold invasions and defeats in the days before the two captivities were

[4] *si obi so,*
[5] Jeremiah 26:16.

only foretelling what many political observers had no doubt foretold.

During one phase of Israel's history, there seems to have been complete anarchy except for sporadic prophets who acted as 'judges', presumably settling disputes while possessed as well as dictating the strategy of warfare.

Naturally there were charlatans, or 'false prophets', who 'prophesied out of their own hearts' without either possession, dreams or hallucinations. Some would fake a spirit-driven run into the bush. 'I sent not these prophets yet they ran: I spake not unto them yet they prophesied.'[6] Moses is uncompromising in his condemnation of false prophets. 'But the prophet which shall speak a word presumptuously in my name, which I have not commanded him to speak, or that shall speak in the name of other gods, that same prophet shall die. And if thou say in thine heart, How shall we know the word which the Lord hath not spoken ? When a prophet speaketh in the name of the Lord, if the thing follow not, nor come to pass, that is the thing which the Lord hath not spoken; the prophet hath spoken it presumptuously: thou shalt not be afraid of him.'[7]

Let us now examine the accounts of some of the Old Testament prophets.

ENOCH: The earliest figure whom we can suspect of spirit possession is Enoch, though he is not explicitly called a prophet. 'And Enoch walked with God; and he was not; for God took him.'[8] This could well mean that he was *physically* made to walk by God and that God took him away into the bush whence he never returned. This is certainly known to happen in Ashanti. I was also told by a Muslim from a remote Northern tribe on the Sahara border of an acquaintance of his who was taken by the spirit into the bush, where he stayed for five years and then returned. I asked what spirit took him and was told, in the exact phrase used of Enoch, 'God took him.'

---

[6] Jeremiah 23:21. Professor Dorothy Emmet takes a rather different view of false prophets: 'Prophets and their Societies', *J. Roy. Anth. Inst.*, vol. LXXXV.

[7] Deuteronomy 18:20–22.

[8] Genesis 5:24.

This Muslim eventually returned and that is what is always hoped of everyone who is 'taken' into the bush. His friends go on believing that he is alive. This apparently was believed of Enoch for so long that the story grew up that he never died and a much later writer says, 'By faith Enoch was translated that he should not see death; and he was not found, because God translated him.'[9]

MOSES: Moses as a prophet is of special interest to anyone who has seen an Ashanti priest conducting *abisa* (consultation) at the door of his sanctuary. Moses did exactly this at the door of the 'tent of meeting', where the supplicants brought their problems and 'Moses brought their cause before the Lord.'[10] Moses seems to have used hallucinogenic fumes to help him to hear the voice of his god. 'And it came to pass when Moses entered into the tent the pillar of cloud descended and stood at the door of the tent: and the Lord spake with Moses . . . and the Lord spake unto Moses face to face, as a man speaketh unto his friend.'[11] Moses did not admit Aaron into the secret of the fumes: 'And the Lord said unto Moses, speak unto Aaron thy brother, that he come not at all times into the holy place within the veil, before the mercy seat which is upon the ark; that he die not; for I will appear in the cloud upon the mercy seat.'[12] On one occasion the fumes were too thick for safety. 'And Moses was not able to enter into the tent of meeting because the cloud abode thereon.'[13] On another occasion Moses employed the same fumes to induce not hallucination but dissociation in no fewer than seventy elders whom he set round about the tent. 'And the Lord came down in the cloud and spake unto him and took of the spirit that was upon him and put it upon the seventy elders: and it came to pass that when the spirit rested upon them they prophesied, but they did so no more.' Two other men who remained in the camp on this emotional occasion were spontaneously possessed, 'and the

9 Hebrews 11:5.
10 Numbers 27:2, 5.
11 Exodus 33:9–11.
12 Leviticus 16:2.
13 Exodus 40:35.

spirit rested upon them . . . and they prophesied in the camp',[14] to the indignation of Joshua, who was astonished that Moses was not jealous of his prophetic monopoly.

The secret of the potent fumes died with Moses, though incense was used in the 'oracle' of Solomon's temple. It seems likely that the gas used by Moses was impure nitrous oxide, obtained by sprinkling ammonium nitrate on a hot, but not red-hot, metal dish. This would explain the fate of the two meddle-some sons of Aaron, who offered unto the Lord strange fire which he had not commanded and died in an explosion. Ammonium nitrate does explode if overheated. 'And Nadab and Abihu, the sons of Aaron, took each of them his censer and put fire therein and laid incense thereon and offered strange fire before the Lord, which he had not commanded them. And there came forth fire from before the Lord and devoured them: and they died before the Lord.'[15]

The harmless nature of nitrous oxide compared with the hallucinogenic fumes of poisonous mushrooms would account for the fact that Moses lived to be very old and 'his eye was not dim nor his natural force abated'.[16] whereas the Delphic Sibyls always died young.

It is permissible to speculate on the source of the jealously guarded secret of the fumes.

At first sight it seems likely that Moses, said to have been 'instructed in all the wisdom of the Egyptians',[17] was taught about ammonium nitrate in Egypt, where ammonium com-pounds were certainly known.[18] But no stores of ammonium nitrate have ever been found in excavated Egyptian temples. It is therefore more probable that Moses's teachers were the Arab-taught priests who initiated Moses into the secrets of Jehovah worship during his forty-day sojourn on the mount. The Arabs

[14] Numbers 11:25, 26.
[15] Leviticus 10:1, 2.
[16] Deuteronomy 34:7.
[17] Acts 7:22.
[18] The word *ammonia* is said to be derived from *Amon*, the court-yard of whose temple always had the ammoniacal smell of the pilgrims' horses.

were among the earliest chemists and certainly 'the work of the apothecary' figured in the new tabernacle ritual.[19]

We should here recall the circumstances in which Moses started to use fumes.

After crossing the Sea of Weeds (the Gulf of Akaba, mistranslated the Red Sea) Moses led his party of migrants straight to the active volcano Horeb,[20] where he had first encountered the angel who gave him his mandate to lead the Israelites to the volcano, there to convert them to the worship of the volcano-god, Jehovah. When they reached the volcano it was in a terrifying state of threatening eruption. 'And it came to pass on the third day, when it was morning, that there were thunders and lightnings, and a thick cloud upon the mount, and the voice of a trumpet exceeding loud; and all the people that were in the camp trembled . . . And mount Sinai was altogether on smoke, because the Lord descended upon it in fire, and the smoke thereof ascended as the smoke of a furnace; and the whole mount quaked greatly . . . Moses spake and God answered him by a voice [volcanic rumbling] . . . and the Lord said unto him . . . Let not the priests and the people break through to come up unto the Lord, lest he break forth upon them.'[21] 'And all the people saw the thunderings and the lightnings, and the voice of the trumpet, and the mountain smoking: and when the people saw it, they trembled, and stood afar off.'[22]

Moses then takes a party of elders to look down into the crater. 'Then went up Moses, and Aaron, Nadab, and Abihu, and seventy of the elders of Israel; and they saw the God Israel: and there was under his feet as it were a paved work of sapphire stone, and as it were the very heaven for clearness. And upon

---

[19] There is no *record* that the early Arabs knew ammonium nitrate and its properties. This is consistent with the intense secrecy always observed concerning sacred medications.

[20] In some of the narratives this mountain is called Sinai. Sinai, however, is far away from Horeb and is not volcanic. Horeb must be a part of the volcanic range running down the eastern seaboard of the Gulf of Akaba.

[21] Exodus 19:16, 18, 19, 24.

[22] Exodus 20:18.

the nobles of the children of Israel he laid not his hand: and they beheld God, and did eat and drink.'[23] It is clear from this passage that the volcano is not simply one of the great works of the creator, it is the god himself.

Then 'the Lord', who is no doubt some 'angel' or priest of Jehovah, gives Moses his ultimate initiation and instructions. 'And he said unto Moses . . . Moses alone shall come near the Lord . . . And Moses rose up and his minister Joshua . . . And Moses was in the mount forty days and forty nights.'

Very long and detailed instructions are given to Moses concerning a beautifully designed and richly furnished tabernacle of testimony. 'At the door of the tent of meeting before the Lord, where I will meet you, to speak there unto thee and there I will meet with the children of Israel.'[24] The tabernacle is duly built and sessions of 'testimony' begin before its door.

The key figure in the secret of the fumes seems to have been the young man Joshua, Moses's personal 'minister' and probably fume technician. It was he alone who accompanied Moses on his forty-day secret initiation. It was he alone who was allowed in the tabernacle when Moses was prophesying in the fumes. 'And it came to pass, when Moses entered into the tent, the pillar of cloud descended and stood at the door of the tent and the Lord spake with Moses. And all the people saw the pillar of cloud stand at the door of the tent: and all the people rose up and worshipped, every man at his tent door. And the Lord spake unto Moses, face to face, as a man speaketh unto his friend. And he turned again into the camp: but his minister Joshua, the son of Nun, a young man, departed not out of the tent.'[25] And it also seems significant that Joshua alone was given a new Jehovah theophorous name: 'And Moses called Hoshea the son of Nun Joshua.'[26] Furthermore, it was Joshua who was indignant when Moses allowed the seventy elders to breathe the fumes.

As has been said, small sub-toxic doses of anaesthetics—

[23] Exodus 24:9–11.
[24] Exodus 29:42, 43.
[25] Exodus 33:9–11.
[26] Numbers 13:16.

insufficient to cause unconsciousness—are sometimes used in Europe to produce hypnosis, a variant of dissociation closely related to that seen in 'spirit possession'. Nitrous oxide varies greatly in its effect on different people and it may well be that its effect on Moses—that producing a hallucinatory voice—was unusual and was a surprise to the Jehovah priests who initiated him. Nevertheless they accepted the voice as a divine manifestation. Later, when the seventy elders were exposed to the fumes they all displayed the more usual phenomena of dissociation and 'prophecy'.

Although Moses went up into the mount for a forty-day period, there is no suggestion that he was 'driven' there.

His final departure to die alone also seems deliberate. 'And the Lord spake unto Moses, saying: Get thee up into this mountain . . . and die in the mount whither thou goest up . . . So Moses died there in the land of Moab according to the word of the Lord and he [the Lord] buried him . . . but no man knoweth of his sepulchre unto this day.'[27]

It is held by some scholars that Moses was murdered. He was certainly threatened with stoning often enough. But even if that occurred it does not detract from the interesting fact that it was *expected* of a prophet that he should go off into the wilderness to die. We shall return to this point later.

BALAAM: Balaam was a soothsayer and divined for money—we do not know by what method. But we are told of one occasion when an awe-inspiring sight threw him into an emotion which brought on a bout of spirit possession. 'When Balaam saw that it pleased the Lord to bless Israel, he went not, as at other times, to meet with enchantments, but he set his face toward the wilderness. And Balaam lifted up his eyes and he saw Israel dwelling according to their tribes, and the spirit of God came upon him.'[28] He then broke into one of those ecstatic psalms of praise which prophets often produced.[29]

[27] Deuteronomy 34:5, 6.
[28] Numbers 24:1, 2.
[29] The poem attributed to Balaam is a paean recited by professional reciters and inserted into the story by later scribes. *Vide* G. B. Gray. *A Critical Introduction to the Old Testament*, London, 1919.

OTHNIEL: The prophets who, during an anarchy lasting 450 years,[30] 'judged Israel' by means of oracular utterances, are an interesting group. They were by no means *only* judges and advisers but were often also forceful men of action.

Of Othniel we are told: 'And when the children of Israel cried unto the Lord, the Lord raised up a saviour to the children of Israel, who saved them, even Othniel, the son of Kenaz, Caleb's younger brother. And the spirit of the Lord came upon him, and he judged Israel; and he went out to war, and the Lord delivered Cushan-rishathaim king of Mesopotamia into his hand, and his hand prevailed against Cushan-rishathaim. And the land had rest forty years. And Othniel the son of Kenaz died.'[31]

DEBORAH: Though women as human beings were of no account, the prophetess Deborah, in her capacity of divine voice, seems to have been accorded full honour and obedience, and 'she judged Israel'. 'And the children of Israel came up to her for judgment. And she sent, and called Barak the son of Abinoam out of Kedeshnaphtali and said unto him: Hath not the Lord, the God of Israel, commanded, saying, Go and draw unto mount Tabor and take with thee ten thousand men of the children of Naphtali, and of the children of Zebulun? And I will draw unto thee to the river Kishon, Sisera, the captain of Jabin's army, with his chariots and his multitude and I will deliver him into thine hand. And Barak said unto her, If thou wilt go with me, then I will go; but if thou wilt not go with me, I will not go. And she said, I will surely go with thee: notwithstanding the journey that thou takest shall not be for thine honour; for the Lord shall sell Sisera into the hand of a woman. And Deborah arose and went with Barak to Kedesh, and Barak called Zebulun and Naphtali together to Kedesh; and there went up ten thousand men at his feet, and Deborah went up with him.'[32] Then follows an

[30] Acts 13:19.
[31] Judges 3:9-11.
[32] Judges 4:5-10.

account of the campaign, including a revolting act of treachery whereby the enemy's leader was slain. After it, Deborah and Barak sing a long duet of rejoicing.

GIDEON: Gideon was not a regular prophet but received his mandate to conduct a campaign against the oppressing Midianites from an 'angel', who seems to have been a flesh-and-blood man of God.[33] Gideon carried out his instructions, but his authority was not accepted by his own people until they saw for themselves the spirit of the Lord seize him. 'Then all the Midianites and the Amalekites and the children of the east assembled themselves together; and they passed over and pitched in the valley of Jezreel. But the spirit of the Lord came upon Gideon and he blew a trumpet, and Abiezer was gathered together after him, and he sent messengers throughout all Manasseh, and they also were gathered together after him, and he sent messengers unto Asher and unto Zebulun and unto Naphtali; and they came up to meet them.'[34]

JEPHTHAH: Jephthah the Gileadite was already a mighty man of valour, though an outcast, when his people persuaded him to lead a campaign against the Ammonites. At the outset, he was hesitant and parleyed with the enemy; suddenly he was galvanized. 'Then the spirit of the Lord came upon Jephthah and he passed over Gilead and Manasseh and passed over Mizpeh of Gilead and from Mizpeh of Gilead he passed over unto the children of Ammon.'[35] It seems likely that this traverse of Gilead, Manasseh and Mizpeh to the borders of Ammon (some thirty miles) was one of those spectacular cross-country runs sometimes achieved when 'the hand of the Lord' is on the runner. At any rate Jephthah paused at the end of it and made a vow to God. He won his battles, his warriors having probably been much heartened by the sight of the spirit of the Lord upon him, and returned home in triumph to fulfil his vow. No Greek tragedy surpasses the story of this honourable fulfilment. After that, it seems, the spirit came to him when needed, for he 'judged Israel six years'.

[33] See Chapter 4.
[34] Judges: 6:33–35.
[35] Judges 11:29.

SAMSON: Samson illustrates two points made in our preliminary outline of the cardinal features of possession; firstly, that immense feats of strength may be performed when the spirit is in action and secondly, that anxiety can inhibit the process of dissociation just as it can inhibit sleep.

Samson was dedicated to the Lord from the womb, and was only a youth when 'the spirit of the Lord began to move him [drive him hard] in Mahaneh-dan'.[36] One day he met a young lion and 'the spirit of the Lord came mightily upon him and he rent him as he would have rent a kid and he had nothing in his hand'.[37] Against his parents' wishes he married a Philistine girl and then had a quarrel with some Philistine young men who joined with his wife to cheat him. 'And the spirit of the Lord came mightily upon him and he went down to Ashkelon and smote thirty men of them.'[38] Then he had further quarrels with the Philistines which brought them to the verge of war with the whole of Judah. Samson aborted the war when the spirit of the Lord came mightily upon him and caused him to 'smite a thousand men with the jawbone of an ass'. After this he 'judged Israel' for twenty years. At the end of this time he had further clashes with the Philistines, whom he overcame with more feats of strength. At last, a Philistine woman enticed him to reveal what he considered the secret of his strength, namely, his Nazarite's uncut hair. In his sleep the Philistines cut off his hair and he found himself unable to explode into his old outbursts of spirit-given strength. The Philistines overpowered him, blinded him and bound him with brass fetters. But as his hair grew, his confidence returned and one day at a festival he took hold of the two middle pillars of the house and pulled it down upon himself and all his tormentors.

SAMUEL: The prophet Samuel was not a great personality, but illustrates several principles concerning prophets. The first appears when he is a child living in the temple with the old priest Eli. A man of God visits Eli and

[36] Judges 13:25.
[37] Judges 14:5–6.
[38] Judges 14:19.

reproves him for tolerating the conduct of his lecherous sons.
The child Samuel then hears a voice in the night calling upon
him to imitate the man of God, so he too rebukes the old priest.
He is exonerated from blame for this monstrous impertinence
on the ground that he is only speaking the word of the Lord.
The reader later has a sense of poetic justice when in Samuel's
old age he is criticized for the depravity of his own sons.

Samuel 'judged Israel all the days of his life'. He does not
appear ever to have been possessed by the spirit, but built altars,
made sacrifices, and 'went from year to year in circuit to
Beth-el and Gilgal and Mizpah, and judged Israel in all those
places'.[39] He seems also, like Elijah and Elisha, to have occupied the post of tribal rain-maker.[40] He accepted fees for
divining.

Hallucinations are mental projections and Samuel had
nothing of much value to project. His judgment was very poor,
and when the Israelites pestered him to choose and anoint a
king for them he disapproved of the scheme but weakly fell in
with it. He selected Saul, the son of Kish, who had no kingly
merit beyond being an unusually tall and handsome man.
When Saul turned out badly, Samuel projected his own bad
judgment on to God. 'Then came the word of the Lord unto
Samuel, saying, It repenteth me that I have set up Saul to be
king.'[41] Even Samuel's divining is suspect. When he told Saul
that he would meet, near the hill of God, 'a company of
prophets, coming down from the high place with a psaltery and
a tabret and a pipe and a harp', he was probably telling him
only what everybody in the district knew that the prophets
would be doing on that day; no doubt he had also heard the
music.

SAUL: Saul, the son of Kish, was not a prophet in
the sense of being the dedicated mouthpiece of a deity, but
from time to time he was possessed and 'prophesied' in the
same way as did whole companies of 'sons of the prophets' and
other people overcome by emotion at a scene of excitement.

[39] 1 Samuel 7:16.
[40] 1 Samuel 12:18.
[41] 1 Samuel 15:10, 11.

The first occasion was on the day when Samuel anointed him king and told him that he would meet a band of prophets making musical commotion and would 'prophesy' with them. He did, 'and the spirit of God came mightily upon him and he prophesied among them. And it came to pass, when all that knew him beforetime saw that, behold, he prophesied with the prophets, then the people said one to another, What is this that is come unto the son of Kish? Is Saul also among the prophets?'[42] The expression, 'What is this that is *come unto* the son of Kish?', is exactly that which would be used in West Africa.

The next time Saul was possessed the precipitating emotion was anger. Nahash the Ammonite came against Jabesh-gilead and said, 'On this condition will I make a covenant with you, that all your right eyes be put out . . . And the spirit of God came mightily upon Saul when he heard those words, and his anger was kindled greatly. And he took a yoke of oxen and cut them in pieces.'[43]

It was not long before Saul proved so stupid and headstrong that Samuel deposed him and anointed the young David in his place, an act which started that rift which resulted in the separation of Judah and Israel into two kingdoms. Naturally, Saul was aggrieved and furiously jealous of David. 'And the spirit of the Lord departed from Saul, and an evil spirit from the Lord troubled him.' This evil spirit, though soothed by harp music, seems to have come and gone in the familiar possessing bouts, and during them Saul was homicidal towards David. 'And it came to pass on the morrow that the evil spirit from God came upon Saul, and he prophesied in the midst of the house: and David played upon his harp as at other times: and there was a javelin in Saul's hand. And Saul cast the javelin, for he said, I will smite David even to the wall with it. And David avoided out of his presence twice.'[44] Later, David's prowess in war further enraged Saul, he made another murderous attack, and David fled for his life and stayed with

[42] I Samuel 10:10–11.
[43] I Samuel 11:2–7.
[44] I Samuel 18:10–11.

Samuel. While he was there, there occurred one of those wild scenes of contagious possession which do take place from time to time. 'And Saul sent messengers to take David and when they saw the company of the prophets prophesying and Samuel standing as head over them, the spirit of God came upon the messengers of Saul and they also prophesied. And when it was told Saul, he sent other messengers and they also prophesied, and Saul sent messengers again the third time and they also prophesied. Then went he also to Ramah and came to the great well that is in Secu: and he asked and said, Where are Samuel and David ? And one said, behold, they be at Naioth in Ramah. And he went hither to Naioth in Ramah: and the spirit of God came upon him also and he went on and prophesied, until he came to Naioth in Ramah. And he also stripped off his clothes and he also prophesied before Samuel and lay down naked all that day and all that night. Wherefore they say, Is Saul also among the prophets ?'[45]

DAVID: Of David we are told: 'Then Samuel took the horn of oil and anointed him in the midst of his brethren: and the spirit of the Lord came mightily upon David from that day forward.'[46] We are not, however, given descriptions of occasions when David was unmistakably possessed. We suspect it on the occasion when David's wife, Michal, the daughter of Saul, criticized his undignified behaviour, but it is not roundly stated that the spirit was upon him. 'And David danced before the Lord with all his might, and David was girded with a linen ephod. So David and all the house of Israel brought up the ark of the Lord with shouting and with the sound of the trumpet. And as the ark of the Lord came into the city of David, Michal, Saul's daughter, looked out at the window and saw King David leaping and dancing before the Lord; and she despised him in her heart . . . Then David returned to bless his household. And Michal the daughter of Saul came out to meet David and said, How glorious was the king of Israel today, who uncovered himself in the eyes of the handmaids of his servants, as one of the vain fellows shamelessly uncovereth himself! And David

[45] I Samuel 19:20-24.
[46] I Samuel 16:13.

said unto Michal, It was before the Lord, which chose me before thy father and above all his house, to appoint me prince over the people of the Lord, over Israel: therefore will I play before the Lord.'[47]

David himself claims to have composed his psalms while under the influence of the spirit, but we are nowhere told who wrote them down. 'And the sweet psalmist of Israel said, the spirit of the Lord spake by me and his word was in my tongue. The God of Israel said, the Rock of Israel spake to me; one that ruleth over men righteously, that ruleth in the fear of God. And he shall be as the light of the morning when the sun riseth, a morning without clouds, with the tender grass springing out of the earth, through clear shining after rain.'[48]

AHIJAH: Solomon, we learn, followed after strange gods, though not wholly deserting Jehovah. One day one of his officers, Jeroboam, was stopped on the road by the prophet Ahijah, who foretold that because of Solomon's sins his son Rehoboam would lose most of his kingdom to Jeroboam. When this reached Solomon's ears, Jeroboam had to fly for his life to Egypt, but the prophet who started the idea went unscathed being held not *personally* responsible for his dicta.

ELIJAH: The most dramatically splendid of all prophets was Elijah the Tishbite, always in peril of his life for denouncing King Ahab's worship of Baal. Elijah was subject to both the 'word' and the 'spirit' of the Lord but he sometimes took the advice of anonymous angels.[49]

So prone was Elijah to be carried off by the spirit into the bush that his loyal friend Obadiah, governor of Ahab's house, dared not trust him to stay in one place for as long as it took to send a message to Ahab. Obadiah says, 'And now thou sayest, Go tell thy lord, behold, Elijah is here, And it shall come to pass, as soon as I am gone from thee, that the spirit of the Lord shall carry thee whither I know not, and so, when I come and tell Ahab, and he cannot find thee, he shall slay me.'[50] Elijah

[47] Samuel 6:14–16, 20, 21.
[48] 2 Samuel 23:1–4.
[49] 2 Kings 1:3, 15.
[50] 2 Kings 18:11, 12.

assured Obadiah that he would not run off to bush, nor did he. Except under stress of extreme emotion, no one need be possessed if determined against it.

King Ahab meekly obeyed Elijah's order to assemble 'all the children of Israel', and four hundred and fifty prophets of Baal, on mount Carmel. There they held a tremendous wonder-working contest, Elijah no doubt ably assisted by his well-trained band of apprentices or 'sons of the prophets'. Elijah remained unpossessed but the prophets of Baal cried aloud and cut themselves with knives and lancets, as do some possessed shamans to this day. Elijah won the contest, slew the four hundred and fifty prophets of Baal, and then carried out a rain-making ceremony. This, too, was successful and rain began to threaten.[51] 'And he said, Go up, say unto Ahab, make ready thy chariot and get thee down, that the rain stop thee not. And it came to pass in a little while that the heaven grew black with clouds and wind and there was a great rain. And Ahab rode and went to Jezreel. And the hand of the Lord was on Elijah, and he girded up his loins and ran before Ahab to the entrance of Jezreel.'[52] From Carmel to Jezreel is some thirty miles, but the 'hand of the Lord' enabled him to keep ahead of Ahab's chariot. No rest awaited him in Jezreel, for Ahab's wife Jezebel was after him and he fled for his life another ninety miles to Beersheba and then a further day's journey into the wilderness, where at last he 'sat down under a juniper tree and requested for himself that he might die'. However, restored by two days' sleep and two meals, 'he went in the strength of that meat forty days and forty nights to Horeb the mount of God', another 200 miles.

So let us hear no more from psychiatrists about dissociation being the prerogative of feeble shirkers and hysterical person-alities.

On Horeb Elijah stayed in a cave[53] and had conversations

---

[51] It was Elijah himself who had fixed the day of the Carmel assembly. No doubt he had already noted signs of approaching rain.

[52] 1 Kings 18:44–46.

[53] It would be interesting to explore the caves on Horeb. They

with the Lord. It appears highly likely that this Lord was one of the angels who seem to have haunted the holy mount. There could well have been a resident community of holy men inhabiting Horeb's caves and receiving as guests such pilgrims as Elijah. The talks Elijah had in the cave were matter-of-fact. The 'still small voice' after the storm was not, according to the modern versions, a voice at all, but a 'low murmuring sound'. Currents of air often produce such sounds in caves. I recall an occasion on which some African friends took me to see a cave near the Volta River. We were standing at the entrance, which was low and uninviting, when a moaning saxophone-like sound came from within, causing all my guides to bolt.

Elijah stayed on Horeb till 'the Lord' ordered him home again. There the end of Elijah was in the tradition of Moses, who deliberately went off to die in solitude, after appointing a successor. A party of fifty sons of the prophets assembled to watch Elijah be 'taken' away, as he had often been 'taken' before. The precipitating emotion was caused by the appearance of a chariot. Elijah and Elisha were walking along, presumably on the road, and talking, when a chariot, seemingly of brightly polished metal, for it is called a chariot of fire, appeared and drove between them. 'And Elijah went up by a whirlwind into heaven.' This could well have happened: I have myself seen an equally sudden whirlwind on a bright sunny day take the roof of a house up to heaven, but the whirlwind was more likely another precipitating factor in the 'taking' of Elijah to bush and into the dust of it he disappeared. This was not the first time that a chariot excited 'the hand of the Lord' to come upon Elijah. The whirlwind was probably not a very strong one, for it dropped Elijah's cloak almost at once. Elisha went back to the fifty sons of the prophets. These men wanted to send out a search party (as would be done in Ashanti today), but Elisha, possibly not wanting to be deprived of his new seniority, was against this. (We have other evidence that he was pettily vain: he cursed some youths who taunted him with being bald

---

might well reveal signs of a monastic community of 'angels' inhabiting the holy mount.

instead of being the 'hairy man' that a prophet was expected to be.) But the sons of the prophets insisted. 'And they said unto him, behold now, there be with thy servants fifty strong men; let them go, we pray thee and seek thy master, lest peradventure the spirit of the Lord hath taken him up and cast him upon some mountain or into some valley. And he said, Ye shall not send. And when they urged him till he was ashamed, he said, Send. They sent therefore fifty men and they sought three days, but found him not.'[54]

ELISHA: Elisha was not so readily possessed as Elijah. Doubtless he had this in mind when he said to the departing Elijah, 'I pray thee, let a double portion of thy spirit be upon me.'[55] Elijah replied that he had no power over this. Certainly Elisha was not able to be possessed at will and had to have musical assistance. When two kings came to consult him he said, 'But now bring me a minstrel. And it came to pass, when the minstrel played, that the hand of the Lord came upon him.'[56] On one occasion Elisha seems to have arrogated to himself a privilege which at all other times has appeared to belong exclusively to angels—he brings satisfaction to the barren Shunamite woman whose husband was old.[57]

### The Later Prophets

The later prophets have nothing to add to our knowledge of prophetic method. The gorgeous heavenly visions which the medications of the Babylonian angels brought about for Ezekiel, Daniel, Zechariah and Esdras were for their private edification and had no direct effect on their mode of prophesying. We are told that the word of the Lord came to them and they certainly produced chapter after chapter of superb poetry, often indicative of alternating moods of deep dejection and sublime joy, but we have virtually no objective narrative

54 2 Kings 2:16–17.
55 2 Kings 2:9.
56 2 Kings 3:15.
57 2 Kings 4:14–17.

concerning their observed behaviour except that of Jeremiah. He was never moved by the spirit of the Lord but the word of the Lord dictated to him so many prophesies of doom concerning the fate of Jerusalem at the hands of Babylon that he was flung into prison by King Zedekiah for spreading alarm and despondency. 'And in the dungeon there was no water but mire: so Jeremiah sank in the mire.' Later he was drawn out by cords and put into the court of the prison where he stayed till Jerusalem was taken by Babylon. Though Nebuchadnezzar slew Zedekiah's sons before his eyes, blinded him, and carried him in chains to Babylon, he treated Jeremiah with great respect, released him from prison and gave him the choice of accompanying the captives of Babylon or staying with the 'remnant' of peasantry left in Judah.

We must wait for the New Testament to show us the spirit of the Lord once more in full activity. In the New Testament the Hebrew *ruach* becomes the Greek *pneuma*, also meaning air or breath, but translated 'the Holy Ghost'.

Part IV

# NEW TESTAMENT ANGELS AND PROPHETS

# 9 The New Testament Angels

*The Babylonian order of angels*

The secret society of seven very holy men, that flourished in Persia, Babylon and Assyria in the days of the captivity, was still persisting some seven hundred years later and was active in Palestine. One of its members, Gabriel, appears in the opening pages of Luke's gospel. Furthermore, we find this Gabriel engaged in one of the earliest recorded activities of holy men, that of bringing pregnancy to the grieving barren wife of an old man.

It is true that myths of the miraculous births of heroes are widespread but there is much in the account of Mary and her cousin Elisabeth which has a firm ring of truth.

Elisabeth is the childless wife of an aged and righteous priest, Zacharias. One day whilst Zacharias is burning incense in his temple in the hill country, an angel comes and tells him that Elisabeth will bear a son, who is to be called John and is to be brought up as a prophet. He says his own name is Gabriel and that he 'stands in the presence of God'. (This presumably means that he partakes from time to time of the heavenly visions of Babylonia and Patmos.) Zacharias is overcome with awe and fear, but nevertheless betrays some incredulity. At this the angel tells him that as a proof of his divine authority he will strike Zacharias dumb until such time as events shall prove him right. Zacharias immediately becomes dumb and when he emerges from the temple to address the congregation outside he cannot speak and has to make signs.

In due time it becomes clear that Elisabeth is with child.

Six months after Gabriel's visit to Zacharias, he visits Elisabeth's cousin Mary, a virgin betrothed to one Joseph of Nazareth. He tells her that she is to bear a holy son and name him Jesus. She protests that she is a virgin but the angel says,

'The Holy Ghost shall come upon you.' No doubt that is what happens and in a state of dissociation she is impregnated by the holy man and afterwards has a genuine amnesia for that part of the encounter.

Before departing, Gabriel tells Mary that Elisabeth is pregnant and as soon as Mary discovers that she also is in this state she hurries into the hill country to tell her cousin. During the utterance of her arrival greeting, Elisabeth's babe 'leapt in her womb' and in the joy and excitement 'Elisabeth was filled with the Holy Ghost'. This had no doubt happened to her before on the occasion of the fruitful visit of Gabriel.

There is thus no need to suppose that either Elisabeth or Mary was *consciously* unfaithful to her husband.

Mary stays three months with Elisabeth, and after her departure Elisabeth is delivered of a son. Eight days later, amid due rejoicing, the child is circumcized and named. Zacharias is still in a state of hysterical aphonia, and when asked to endorse the somewhat foreign name of John, he can communicate only on a writing tablet. His approval of the name causes so much marvelling that 'his mouth was opened immediately and his tongue loosed'.

Zacharias himself then becomes filled with the Holy Ghost and utters prophecies.[1]

A further—and more tentative—speculation may be made concerning this angel Gabriel. Was he the same one who announced to the Bethlehem shepherds the birth of Mary's child ? As an itinerant he might well have chanced to be in Bethlehem, to have felt gratified to hear of the birth, and, coming upon the shepherds, whom his nocturnal arrival and his holy man's insignia startled, have told them not to be frightened as he had only good news.

'And there were shepherds in the same country abiding in the field keeping watch by night over their flock and an angel of the Lord stood by them and the glory of the Lord shone round about them and they were sore afraid. And the angel said unto them, Be not afraid, for behold, I bring you good tidings of

[1] Luke 1:5-67.

great joy, which shall be to all the people. For there is born to you this day, in the city of David, a saviour, which is Christ the Lord. And this is the sign unto you, Ye shall find a babe wrapped in swaddling clothes and lying in a manger. And suddenly there was with the angel a multitude of the heavenly host praising God and saying, Glory to God in the highest and on earth peace among men in whom he is well pleased.'[2]

The important point to notice here is the sharp distinction between the itinerant holy man—the angel who talked with the shepherds—and the 'heavenly host', which latter is the only supernatural embellishment of the story. Where the Gospel tells us that 'the glory of the Lord shone about them', the Greek word *doxa*, translated 'glory', does not mean physical splendour but honour, credit or reputation, and the passage seems to mean that the holy man carried the awe-inspiring authority of his calling, which we have already seen was one of the assets of itinerant angels.

We are told a little later that 'all that heard it wondered at the things which were spoken unto them by the shepherds. But Mary kept all these sayings, pondering them in her heart.'[3] We are entitled to think that she might have identified the angel described by the shepherds with the one who had visited her.

### The other New Testament angels

We have already observed the behaviour of the itinerant angel Gabriel who visited Zacharias, Elisabeth, Mary and probably also the shepherds. He clearly belongs to the Babylonian–Assyrian–Persian cult which flourished at the time of the captivities in Assyria and Babylon. We have also seen that the angel who administered an hallucinogenic medication to St John the Divine on the Isle of Patmos was very closely following another tradition of that cult.

2 Luke 2:8–14.
3 Luke 2:18, 19.

It is also noticeable that the New Testament Gabriel resembles in another respect the very much older angels who brought pregnancy to the wives of Abram and Manoah. We must suppose that the Babylonian order had very ancient fore-runners.

But there seems to have been another and very different *genre* of angels who were friends of the prophet Jesus. It would indeed have been surprising if Jesus, who spent all the time he could in solitary places alone, had not made friends with any unworldly simple-minded holy men he met there.

At the outset of his ministry, when Jesus was spending the traditional forty days in the wilderness, he was helped and fed by angels, reminding us of Elijah under the juniper tree.

'Then was Jesus led up of the spirit into the wilderness to be tempted of the devil. And when he had fasted forty days and forty nights, he afterward hungered . . . Then the devil leaveth him and, behold, angels came and ministered unto him.'[4]

On the night of his arrest in the garden of Gethsemane,[5] an angel came and 'strengthened' him. This assertion pre-sumably rests on the witness of the disciples, who were also in the garden and had failed in the same office.

'And he went forward a little, and fell on his face, and prayed, saying, O my Father, if it be possible, let this cup pass away from me: nevertheless not as I will, but as thou wilt. And he cometh unto the disciples and findeth them sleeping and saith unto Peter, What, could ye not watch with me one hour ?'[6]

'And there appeared unto him an angel from heaven, strengthening him.'[7]

We are entitled to wonder whether this angel was the same young man, religiously garbed in linen, who followed the escort after the disciples had fled. 'And a certain young man followed with him, having a linen cloth cast about him, over his naked

[4] Matthew 4:1, 2, 11.
[5] Luke sets this scene on the mount of Olives, the other evangelists in a garden.
[6] Matthew 26:39, 40.
[7] Luke 22:43.

body, and they lay hold on him: but he left the linen cloth and fled naked.'[8]

And was this the same young man in white who hung around the empty sepulchre and took the message about Jesus having gone to Galilee? 'And entering into the tomb, they saw a young man sitting on the right side arrayed in a white robe; and they were amazed. And he said unto them, Be not amazed: ye seek Jesus the Nazarene, which hath been crucified: he is risen; he is not here: behold the place where they laid him. But go, tell his disciples and Peter, he goeth before you into Galilee: there shall ye see him, as he said unto you.'[9]

Finally, was this young man one of the two who turned up in white at the last assembly with Jesus on Olivet? 'And while they looked stedfastly into heaven as he went, behold, two men stood by them in white apparel, which also said, Ye men of Galilee, why stand ye looking into heaven? This Jesus, which was received up from you into heaven, shall so come in like manner as ye beheld him going into heaven.'[10]

After the departure of Jesus there was still some association between his disciples and the local angels. An angel arranged a meeting between Philip and Queen Candace's eunuch. 'And an angel of the Lord spake unto Philip, saying, Arise and go toward the south, unto the way that goeth down from Jerusalem unto Gaza; the same is desert. And he arose and went and behold, a man of Ethiopia, an eunuch of great authority under Candace, queen of the Ethiopians, who was over all her treasure, who had come to Jerusalem for to worship, was returning, and sitting in his chariot, reading the prophet Isaiah. And the spirit said unto Philip, Go near and join thyself to this chariot.'[11]

An angel also arranged a meeting between Peter and Cornelius the centurion. We are told that the angel came 'in a vision', but Cornelius himself calls him a man. 'And Cornelius said, Four days ago until this hour, I was keeping the ninth hour of prayer in my house and, behold, a man stood

---

8 Mark 14:50–52.
9 Mark 16:5–7.
10 Acts 1:10, 11.
11 Acts 8:26–29.

before me in bright apparel. And said, Cornelius, thy prayer is heard and thine alms are had in remembrance in the sight of God. Send therefore to Joppa and call unto thee Simon, who is surnamed Peter; he is lodged in the house of Simon a tanner by the sea side.'[12]

Another friendly angel seems to have robbed the imprisoned Peter's sleeping guards of their keys. (Anyone who has observed how the native police of a colonial power do behave on night watch will have no doubt that Peter's guards were sound asleep.) 'And when Herod was about to bring him forth, the same night Peter was sleeping between two soldiers, bound with two chains: and guards before the door kept the prison. And, behold, an angel of the Lord stood by him and a light shined in the cell: and he smote Peter on the side and awoke him, saying, Rise up quickly. And his chains fell off from his hands. And the angel said unto him, Gird thyself and bind on thy sandals, and he did so. And he saith unto him, Cast thy garment about thee and follow me. And he went out and followed him, and wist not that it was true which was done by the angel, but thought he saw a vision. When they were past the first and the second ward, they came unto the iron gate that leadeth unto the city, which opened to them of its own accord, and they went out and passed on through one street; and forthwith the angel departed from him.'[13]

In the light of the recent flood of illumination which has come from the Dead Sea researches, the obvious conclusion concerning the New Testament angels (always excepting the older Babylonian order) is that they were Essenes.

It is no part of my task to reproduce new and old knowledge concerning the Essenes, but a few facts relevant to our enquiry must be mentioned.

The Essenes were a sect of pre-Christian Gnostics who lived monastic lives.[14] The bulk of our knowledge of them comes

---

[12] Acts 10:30–32.

[13] Acts 12:6–10.

[14] F. Legge, *Forerunners and Rivals of Christianity*, Cambridge, 1915, and a very large number of later works.

from Philo of Alexander writing about AD 20 and Josephus about AD 70. Pliny also, in his *Natural History*, speaks very briefly of the Essenes and he locates their monastery exactly where recent excavations have, indeed, unearthed it.

Josephus says that the Essenes were one of three 'philosophic' sects, the Pharisees and the Saducees being the other two. He describes the Essenes—whose name is thought to mean 'the Pure' or 'the Pious'—as a small sect, totalling not more than four thousand, scattered throughout the villages of Palestine. They lived entirely by manual labour, practised community of goods, celibacy and charity, and wore white garments. They abstained from temple worship because they disapproved of the sacrifice of living animals and they partook of a sacramental meal.[15] Their inner circle had a great deal of secret literature, secret rites and secret knowledge.

After the discovery of the first Dead Sea scrolls in a cave in 1947, all the neighbouring caves were explored and thirty-seven of them were found to contain pottery and other signs of human occupancy, suggesting that the community began as a primitive association of hermits.[16]

As early as 1876, such scholars as Bishop J. B. Lightfoot believed that Jesus and John the Baptist derived much of their doctrine from the Essenes. Documents recently discovered reveal that an Essene called the Teacher of Righteousness, who was martyred about 65–53 BC was the prototype of Jesus, preaching penitence, poverty, humility and love, but also fiercely insisting, as did Jesus, that the wicked would be cast into hell fire.

At any rate it seems likely that Jesus and his disciples had friends among the Essenes, and that some of these were the

---

[15] In George Moore's great novel *The Brook Kerith* (1916) there is an imaginative but soundly based description of Essene monastic life.

[16] Edmund Wilson, *The Scrolls from the Dead Sea*, London, 1957; Theodore H. Gaster, *The Scriptures of the Dead Sea Sect*, London, 1957; A. Dupont-Sommer, *The Essene Writings from Qumran*, Oxford, 1961; G. Vermes, *The Dead Sea Scrolls in English*, London, 1962.

angels who appear from time to time in the New Testament narratives.

Whether there was any association between the Essenes and the Babylonian order of angels who appear in the New Testament, we do not know; but if we assume that this was so it explains one point which has puzzled the earlier students of the Essenes. This is Josephus's statement that the Essenes were sworn to secrecy as to 'the names of the angels'. The scholars, who saw no reason why any Jew should wish to keep secret the well-known names Michael and Gabriel, were driven to postulating that the Essenes used the names of the angels for magical purposes in exorcising demons and healing diseases.[17] This might be plausible if all angels were ethereal visitants from the sky, as the scholars supposed, but if they were flesh-and-blood holy men, who did in fact keep their personal names secret, as the Old Testament often asserts and Revelation suggests, then the explanation is a much simpler one.

[17] F. Legge, *op. cit.*

# 10 The Spirit of the Lord in the New Testament

*The Prophet John the Baptist*

As we have seen, John was consecrated from before his birth and an itinerant man of God ordered that he was to be brought up as a prophet. This exactly repeats the story of the birth of Samson. The man of God, Gabriel, foretold that John would go forth 'in the spirit and power of Elias', but we have no evidence that either the 'spirit of the Lord' or the 'word of the Lord' ever came to him. However, he took his dedication seriously and 'was in the deserts till the day of his shewing unto Israel'. He ate locusts and wild honey, wore the traditional prophet's leathern girdle, denounced wickedness, preached repentance, elicited confessions, had a company of sons of the prophets or disciples, and baptized penitents with water in the sacred river, Jordan.

*The Prophet Jesus*

Jesus was a kinsman of John, maybe a half-brother, and they much admired one another, despite a great difference in natural endowment. John had little but a fiery courageous earnestness. Jesus was of commanding intellectual stature, besides being a great religious genius. At the age of thirty, Jesus began his prophet's career by being baptized by John. The emotional experience of baptism threw him into a state of dissociation and he was driven away into the bush for the traditional forty days in the manner of Elijah and many a driven Ashanti novice today. 'And straightway coming up out of the water, he saw the heavens rent asunder and the Spirit as a dove descending upon him: and a voice came out of the heavens, Thou art my beloved Son, in thee I am well pleased. And straightway the Spirit driveth him forth into the wilderness. And he was in the wilderness forty days.'[1]

The dove may well have been an ordinary one. Doves do blunder about and when they do so some supernatural significance is usually attached to them, for they are sacred birds in many countries. On one occasion in Africa a dove crashed into the radiator of my car. Later when the car broke down, this was attributed to the dove. Other birds too are often credited with supernatural significance. I recall a supplicant who came to a shrine complaining that a bird had flown into her room. The voice from heaven was almost certainly thunder, for we are told of another New Testament occasion when 'a voice out of heaven' was heard and 'the multitude therefore that stood by and heard it said that it had thundered'.[2]

The importance of Jesus's forty days in the wilderness lies not in the emotional crisis of dissociation that drove him there— dissociation in itself is no more elevating or degrading than is sleep—but in his decision to embark upon the dedicated career which the baptism inaugurated. We know that at the age of twelve he had astonished learned men by his doctrine, and no doubt he had continued reflecting on 'all the kingdoms of the world and the glory of them'—and the vanity of them. We know also that throughout the next eighteen years he was a great religious mystic who lived in very close communion with his heavenly father—so close that he was able to say, 'I and my father are one.' These facts, together with the quality of his teaching, determine the status of Jesus among prophets. The one short episode of dissociation is unimportant.

Throughout his ministry, Jesus referred to himself as the Son of Man, as other prophets had done before him, and immediately after his ministry, before the advent of Pauline Trinitarian theology, his disciples described him simply as 'a prophet mighty in word and deed' and 'a man approved of God among you'.

[1] Mark 1:10-13.
[2] John 12:28, 29.

The end of the life of Jesus also runs true to the tradition of the great prophets. The idea that he died on the cross is acceptable only by those nurtured on the Pauline doctrine of resurrection.[3] He was on the cross but a few hours, whereas crucifixion was a slow death, the victim usually dying on the *third or fourth day*. He was no doubt deeply unconscious and Joseph of Arimathea and the centurion may well have been in good faith when they assured the incredulous Pilate that he was dead.[4] At any rate he did revive when laid flat. Then he spent a further ritual period of forty days, elusively, in the wilderness, but sometimes joined his friends at dusk or dawn to take food. He looked—as very sick people often do—so much changed that his friends hardly knew him. Then 'when forty days were fulfilled' he gathered his disciples on a hillside, as the sons of the prophets had been gathered to take farewell of Elijah. In the act of blessing them, he was 'taken up'. The Greek word *eperthē* (translated 'taken up') has a great many meanings besides that of being physically lifted. It also means 'stirred up, roused, excited or elated'.[5] There is no reason to suppose that the evangelists[6] wished to convey a picture of Jesus soaring through the air into the sky. They were quite familiar, as European biblical scholars are not, with the phenomenon of dissociation. They can be faithfully interpreted as meaning that Jesus was 'taken' by the spirit of the Lord as he had been 'taken' at the outset of his ministry and as earlier prophets had often been 'taken', and that he ran swiftly up the hillside into a hill-top mist or cloud. It was not new for prophets to disappear into a

---

3 Paul's doctrine is itself an adaptation of ancient pagan ideas. The best account of these is, to this day, Franz Cumont's great classic, *Oriental Religions in Roman Paganism*.

4 The reader may recall the case of a woman who, in England in 1969, was declared by a doctor to be dead and was taken to the mortuary where she began to revive. She made a perfect recovery.

5 Liddell and Scott, *Greek/English Lexicon*, Oxford.

6 All the accounts of the 'ascension' except that in the Acts are designated by scholars 'rejected readings', that is, interpolations containing important matter apparently derived from extraneous sources.

cloud on foot without flying through the air. 'And Moses entered into the midst of the cloud and went up into the mount.'[7] We learn, moreover, that some of the spectators firmly insisted that Jesus would come back 'in like manner', just as Africans who have been 'taken' to bush sometimes come back, for he was—unlike Moses and Elijah—but a young man. They forgot, however, that he was a very sick man, for a soldier's spear had pierced his 'side' (*pleura*), probably between the ribs.[8]

Although Jesus preached the revolutionary, simple and profound doctrine of the universal loving fatherhood of God and the coming of the Kingdom of Heaven, he followed, like John, the prophets' tradition of passionately denouncing local wickedness and, like John, he fell into trouble through this.

We have no reason to believe that Jesus was ever dissociated except at the beginning and the end of his ministry, but he did foresee that the euphoria and comfort of possession could sustain his bereft and bewildered followers after his departure and he did encourage them to accept this aid.

*Pentecost and post-Pentecost*

Shortly after the departure of Jesus, at a gathering on the day of Pentecost, there was inaugurated a phase when the spirit was 'poured out' almost 'upon all flesh'.

'And when the day of Pentecost was now come, they were all together in one place. And suddenly there came from heaven a sound as of the rushing of a mighty wind and it filled all the house where they were sitting. And there appeared unto them tongues parting asunder, like as of fire; and it sat upon each one of them. And they were all filled with the Holy Spirit and began to speak with other tongues, as the Spirit gave them

---

[7] Exodus 24:15–18.

[8] That the wound bled is evidence that he was alive. The wound was probably in the chest, for people are able to go about with lung abscesses and other serious lung lesions, but not with damaged abdominal viscera.

utterance. Now there were dwelling at Jerusalem Jews, devout men, from every nation under heaven. And when this sound was heard, the multitude came together and were confounded, because that every man heard them speaking in his own language. And they were all amazed and marvelled, saying, Behold, are not all these which speak Galileans ? And how hear we, every man in our own language, wherein we were born ? Parthians and Medes and Elamites and the dwellers in Mesopotamia, in Judea and Cappadocia, in Pontus and Asia, in Phrygia and Pamphylia, in Egypt and in the parts of Libya about Cyrene, and sojourners from Rome, both Jews and proselytes, Cretans and Arabians, we do hear them speaking in our tongues the mighty works of God. And they were all amazed and were perplexed, saying one to another, What meaneth this ? But others mocking said, They are filled with new wine.'[9]

None of these phenomena is outside fairly common experience. I have myself been in a quiet house when a sudden rush of wind has set all the doors and shutters crashing and carried away the roof. Fireballs and other electrical phenomena are known. Even on Exmoor I have sat in a house and watched an alarming procession of blue sparks steadily crackling down to earth inside a cupboard. Lightning in Africa is notoriously the thing that throws some shamans into their first possession. Glossolalia, and fragments of languages heard in childhood and subsequently forgotten, are also common. It must be remembered that at the annual festivals strangers from far and wide gathered in Jerusalem and no doubt lodged in houses where there were children. No doubt a lodger would return year after year to the same house and the quick-eared Galilean children would pick up his foreign phrases. Though it is probably an exaggeration that the Pentecostal assembly spoke in foreign tongues of 'the mighty works of God', they could well have uttered such phrases as 'God be with you' and 'The blessing of God be upon this house'.

Then began a period when possession spread like an epidemic among the converts to the new faith. It seems to have been general at all assemblies. 'And when they had prayed the place

[9] Acts 2:1–13.

was shaken wherein they were gathered together and they were all filled with the Holy Ghost, and they spake the word of God with boldness.'[10] Baptism, always an emotional experience,[11] was a common occasion for an initial possession, and the laying on of hands was another precipitant.

The narratives stress the striking distinction between those who 'received' the Holy Ghost and those who did not. 'Now when the apostles which were at Jerusalem heard that Samaria had received the word of God, they sent unto them Peter and John: who, when they were come down, prayed for them, that they might receive the Holy Ghost: for as yet he was fallen upon none of them: only they had been baptized into the name of the Lord Jesus. Then laid they their hands on them and they received the Holy Ghost.' Again, to the astonishment of Peter, a group of Gentiles were affected even before they had been baptized. 'While Peter yet spake these words, the Holy Ghost fell on all them which heard the word. And they of the circumcision which believed were amazed, as many as came with Peter, because on the Gentiles was poured out the gift of the Holy Ghost. For they heard them speak with tongues and magnify God. Then answered Peter, Can any man forbid the water that they should not be baptized which have received the Holy Ghost as well as we?' Of another group of believers encountered by Paul we are told: 'And he said unto them, Did ye receive the Holy Ghost when ye believed? And they said unto him, Nay, we did not so much as hear whether the Holy Ghost was given. And he said, Into what then were ye baptized? And they said, into John's baptism. And Paul said, John baptized with the baptism of repentance, saying unto the people that they should believe on him which should come after him, that is, on Jesus. And when they heard this they were baptized into the name of the Lord Jesus. And when Paul laid

[10] Acts 4:31.

[11] The former Archbishop of Canterbury, Dr Fisher, said in a radio interview that the only occasion on which he ever became so much moved as to be near breaking down in public was that of anointing the Queen with oil at the coronation.

his hands on them the Holy Ghost came on them, and they spake with tongues and prophesied.'

The baptism of the eunuch by Philip is remarkable in that Philip was, of the two, the more profoundly moved—moved so literally that he dashed across country in the familiar Ashanti and Hebrew fashion. 'And as they went on the way they came to a certain water and the eunuch saith, Behold here is water, what doth hinder me to be baptized? And he commanded the chariot to stand still, and they both went down into the water, both Philip and the eunuch, and he baptized him. And when they came up out of the water the Spirit of the Lord caught away Philip, and the eunuch saw him no more, for he went on his way rejoicing. But Philip was found at Azotus'[12]—whether after an organized search we are not told.

Philip's aptitude for dissociation was inherited by his 'four daughters, virgins, which did prophesy'.

There can be no doubt about the impetus given to early Christianity by the phenomenon of dissociation, not only through the excitement, the euphoria and the enthusiasm of the dissociated, but also by the conviction and authority which this supposedly supernatural spectacle conveyed to the onlooker.

The phenomenon of 'speaking with tongues', which no doubt means glossolalia or the babbling of meaningless gibberish and baby-talk, very soon began to worry the apostle Paul, though he did his best to tolerate it.[13] 'For he that speaketh in an unknown tongue speaketh not unto men, but unto God, for no man understandeth, but in the spirit he speaketh mysteries. But he that prophesieth speaketh unto men edification, and comfort, and consolation . . . and greater is he that prophesieth than he that speaketh with tongues, except he interpret, that the church may receive edifying. Now, brethren,

---

[12] Acts 8:36-40.

[13] I Corinthians 14. This is one of the passages which the Authorized Version renders more meaningfully than does the New English Bible. The translators of the latter have evidently not witnessed what they term 'ecstatic utterance' and do not know that it can be of two kinds: (a) the novice's meaningless glossolalia or 'unknown tongue', and (b) intelligible prophecy.

if I come unto you speaking with tongues, what shall I profit you ? . . . So also ye, unless ye utter by the tongue speech easy to be understood, how shall it be known what is spoken ? . . . Howbeit in the church I had rather speak five words with my understanding, that I might instruct others also, than ten thousand words in a tongue . . . If therefore the whole church be assembled together and all speak with tongues and there come in men unlearned or unbelieving, will they not say that ye are mad ?[14]

The later Christian prophets owed their extinction to the poverty of their understanding and the consequent inanity of their prophesying. Gibbon writes of the primitive church: 'The want of discipline and human learning was supplied by the occasional assistance of the *prophets*, who were called to that function without distinction of age, of sex, or of natural abilities, and who, as often as they felt the divine impulse, poured out the effusions of the Spirit in the assembly of the faithful. But these extraordinary gifts were frequently abused or misapplied by the prophetic teachers. They displayed them at an improper season, presumptuously disturbed the service of the assembly, and by their pride or mistaken zeal they introduced, particularly into the apostolic Church of Corinth, a long and melancholy train of disorders. As the institution of prophets became useless, their powers were withdrawn and their office abolished.'[15]

In less than two centuries the Church had wholly rejected the Holy Ghost as it was originally conceived and freedom of Christian prophecy became the Montanist Heresy.

[14] 1 Corinthians 14.
[15] Edward Gibbon, *Decline and Fall of the Roman Empire,* chap. XV.

Appendix I

# Latterday Dissociation Cults

*Prophetism in West Africa*

About the year 1910 there appeared in Liberia—where at that time there were no Christian missions—a fervent and un-sophisticated preacher called the Prophet Harris. His theology was simple: he preached the loving fatherhood of God. I do not know whether he was ever possessed by the Holy Ghost or whether his congregations practised possession. His importance is that he was the first of the latterday 'prophets' in West Africa. He preached not only in Liberia but in Freetown, the Ivory Coast and the Gold Coast. He died in 1929.[1]

The fashion of prophet cults was firmly established in the Western Province of the Gold Coast before the nineteen-thirties, when I saw several of them in action in the Axim district. Spirit possession of all the members of the congregation was by then a part of the normal practice. Most of the meetings were held out of doors; they began with healing sessions when sick people came for blessing, and then passed into possession sessions, when the Holy Ghost, amid great excitement, entered the worshippers. One cult was called the Water Carriers. The members stood in a ring round the prophet or prophetess, each holding on his head a basin of water from a holy well. After a little drumming, clapping and singing, the spirit entered each basin of water, the carrier rocked, swayed, quivered and danced in the ancient possessed fashion, and the inspired water slopped over and ran down his body. It was said that virgins sometimes became pregnant by the Holy Ghost: if the prophet leader knew better he said nothing.

[1] I am indebted for these dates to Dr Gordon Haliburton, whose *The Prophet Harris* has recently been published (London, 1971).

Harris's followers and imitators cannot be said to have constituted an organized church. But in the year 1937 the Apostolic Church of Wales sent missionaries to West Africa. This church was an outcome of the Welsh revival of 1905, and held its first large convention in Pen-y-goroes in South Wales in 1916. The members claimed to worship in the manner of the earliest Christians but though the meetings in Wales were informed by intense joyous ardour there is not, so far as I have been able to discover, any evidence that florid dissociation was practised, though 'speaking with tongues' was not unknown. But once the cult arrived in West Africa it took on an African character, spirit possession in the congregation became its cardinal feature and it spread like wildfire. Nigeria has today the largest number of Apostolic churches of any country in the world.[2] In Ghana this church is the second largest in the country, though Christian missions have existed there for centuries.[3]

No sooner was spirit possession established as a permissible feature of organized church worship in West Africa by the Apostolic Church than thousands of other similar new churches exploded into being. Today they recruit their members from two main sources. Firstly, new members come from the long-established Christian churches, whose assemblies are so dull and dreary that Africans could never have tolerated them had they not been, for a long time, the only doorway to education. Secondly, recruits come from the pagan shrines which sprang up and proliferated after the cocoa-boom of the nineteen-twenties, gave worshippers a sense of protection against new dangers, but became so avaricious that they brought many members to poverty. It is now difficult to find in Ghana any village of more than a dozen houses which has not a flourishing assembly of these new Christians. The churches multiply daily,

[2] I am indebted to the central Welsh office of the Apostolic Church for this information.

[3] Dr C. G. Baeta in his *Prophetism in Ghana* (London, 1962) dismisses as unworthy of consideration these communities originated by foreigners. But the important practice of spirit possession, as a permissible feature of church worship, undoubtedly began in West Africa in the Apostolic Church.

mainly by the process of fission, for no sooner does the smallest difference of opinion arise in a church than the dissidents hive off under a new 'prophet'.

The assemblies are all crowded, noisy and joyous, with drumming, clapping, singing and spirit possession. Most of them practise anointing with oil and the laying on of hands, and claim miracles of healing. Some of them have settlements of in-patients staying for treatment. Some 'prophets' combine prophetism with traditional herbalism and their in-patient clinics probably account for the largest number of patients under treatment for mental illness in Ghana today.

The noticeable feature of the members of these churches is their euphoria. This seems to be a direct result of practising the mental mechanism of dissociation regularly but temperately. Ghana today is full of envy, fear and distrust: the lorries which exhibit such slogans as 'Enemies about me' are only expressing the prevalent sentiment. Eighty per cent of the mental illness of Ghana is floridly paranoid, the patients being convinced that people are plotting to kill them.[4] But the members of the new churches are noticeably happier, more generous and less afraid than the rest.

In Ghana membership of the new 'spiritual' churches is by no means confined to rural illiterates. Some of the best educated and the most responsible of Ghanaians are members. The Speaker of the first legislative assembly after the attainment of independence, an elderly, wise and universally respected lawyer, was a member of the Apostolic Church. The first African to be appointed as a bank manager was another.

### The Subud Cult

This cult, now world-wide, began in 1933, when a Muslim Indonesian, now called Pak Subuh, was hit by what seems to have been a fire-ball and fell, for the first time in his life, into the dissociated state. Many more episodes of dissociation came

[4] M. J. Field, 'Chronic Psychosis in Rural Ghana', *British Journal of Psychiatry*, vol. 114, no. 506, January 1968.

upon him during the next few years, and the euphoric contentment that began to inform his life convinced him that he had
received a great spiritual gift which, if it became widespread,
could benefit all mankind. He found that it could be transmitted and that where two or three were gathered together it
was particularly contagious. The meetings held were called
*latihans* or training exercises. It was not claimed that Subud was
a religion or a teaching; simply that it was a religious experience
compatible with the profession of any ethical religion. There
are now thousands of Subud members and centres all over the
world. Britain has many.

Professor V. H. Mottram, a physiologist, has an enthusiastic
epilogue to his book, *The Physical Basis of Personality*,[5] in which
he claims that the Subud experience is the opening up of the
hard shell of the outer personality and the release of the inner
self or divine spark hidden therein. He writes, 'There is a
release from physical and emotional tension leading to a gaiety
of heart and firmness of purpose. Later there may come a real
appraisal, often humiliating, of one's everyday self; this in turn
produces a disappearance of self-will and conceit. There is a
growing consideration for others with a behaviour alien to the
previous self, often to the surprise of the person himself.
Problems are faced no longer with diffidence. The more
advanced feel themselves in touch with a source of wisdom of
which formerly they were unaware.' This is a restatement of the
early Christian claim that 'the fruit of the Spirit is love, joy,
peace, long-suffering, gentleness, goodness, faith'.

There is no doubt about the contented euphoria of those
Subud members who are able to practise twice-weekly dissociation in their *latihan* meetings, and no doubt that this
contentment makes them kinder and more valuable people.
Subud has, however, nothing to offer those who are not able to
become dissociated. They become bored with the meetings and
drop out.

It is certain that what happens in Subud meetings is dissociation. I have myself witnessed some familiar phenomena

[5] V. H. Mottram, *The Physical Basis of Personality*, Penguin, 1952.

and others have been described to me by members. The sexes are segregated at *latihan* meetings because new men members are likely to become violent and have to be restrained, just as possession novices in Africa have to be prevented from rushing off into the bush. In Subud idiom, their aggressions and conflicts are working their way out. Another familiar feature is that only long-practised members are able to speak, though new members may produce glossolalia. As might be expected, assemblies of dissociated British people are quieter than their African counterparts. The unrestrained African dancing is represented by gentle swaying and arm waving, reminiscent of 'eurhythmics', and the singing by harmonious humming, always in a minor key and reminiscent of Highland dirges. As in African spirit possession, the members have to become conditioned to behave in an acceptable way and only experienced members are allowed to practise alone.

It may well be that dissociation, hitherto dismissed as morbid, has a future in psychiatric therapeutics.

Appendix II

# The Background of Moses

It is no part of the business of this study to enter the cockpit where scholars fight out such questions as: Was Moses an Egyptian? Does the book of Hosea indicate that he was murdered by Ephraimites? Was he several leaders condensed into one to simplify a history? Was Quades (Kadesh-Meribah) and not Horeb the scene of the Israelites' initiation into the worship of the volcano-god Jehovah? Who pinned the ubiquitous myth of exposure among the bulrushes on to the Israelites' hero?

But one or two of these matters receive illumination from practices which persist in some communities today, so may be mentioned.

Among these is Moses's Egyptian name. This does not (as Freud supposed) militate against the Hebrew pedigree given in Exodus,[1] a pedigree consistent with the endogamous practice of the lineage of Abraham. This practice was honoured by strict Hebrews right down to the time of the captivity in Assyria.[2]

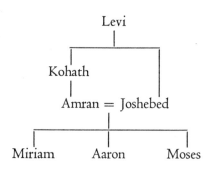

[1] Exodus 6:20.
[2] Tobit 1:9; 7:12.

If anyone still doubts that Miriam, Moses and Aaron were Hebrew siblings, let him read the story of the family row that blew up when Moses married a Cushite woman.[3]

Genesis makes it very clear that the inbred members of Abraham's lineage lived in mortal dread of infertility and it is highly likely that Amran and Joshebed, who were aunt and nephew, as well as wife and husband, went to the shrine of some Egyptian deity and supplicated for a son. Israelites felt no abhorrence of Egyptian gods: Joseph's sons by his marriage to the daughter of a priest of On were unhesitatingly blessed by Jacob and given the same status as his own sons. Amran and Joshebed probably carried out exactly the same procedure as do any West African married couple going to the shrine of any deity of any tribe—the more foreign the deity the greater the power attributed to him. If such a couple subsequently achieve a child they return to render thanks and to be given a theophorous name for it. Thus, a child born after invoking the aid of the deity Kundi or the river-god Pra might be called Kofi Kundi or Abena Pra. The name Moses[4] is the Egyptian equivalent of Theodore, which name specifies no particular deity.

The attribution of the 'drawn-out-of-the-water' meaning is the result of two of the most popular primitive pastimes still to be found actively practised in West Africa. The first is the game of speculating on the meanings of proper names (place-names, however, being commoner topics of discussion than personal names) and the second is the habit of affixing almost universal myths to historic events.[5]

The first is exemplified by the new meaning for the place-name Legon invented by the students of the Ghanaian university now on that site. They believe that it means 'the Hill of Knowledge' (from the Ga le, to know, and gon, a hill). But the

---

[3] Numbers 12.

[4] Ra-mose and Thut-mose are among the better-known Egyptian theophorous names incorporating the word *mose*, a son.

[5] The bulrush myth is also attached to Sargon I, who founded the Akkadian-Sumerian empire, Attis of Phrygia exposed on the banks of the River Sangarius, and many others. The *Ion* of Euripides has an infant exposed in a cradle of reeds.

name in fact dates from a time when a tribe called the Le, whose better informed descendants still exist elsewhere, lived on the hill.

The second is exemplified by the history of a man called Tetteh Quashie, who planted the first successful cocoa-farm in the Gold Coast. His achievement was subsequently embellished by the world-wide myth of a hero who smuggles seeds in a hollow walking-stick. Cocoa was, in fact, introduced into the Gold Coast by the Basel Mission about 1857, and by Governor Sir William Brandford Griffith about 1885.[6]

It is important to note that such myths and meanings are the work of popular hearsay. Tetteh Quashie's own family do not subscribe to the hollow staff myth and the elders of the Le tribe in Kpone and Osudoku know the true history of the Le hill. The contrast between the accuracy of family histories handed down by illiterates whose duty it is to know them, and the wild untruth of the stories bandied about by popular gossip, must always be borne in mind.

Another great event in the story of Moses is illuminated by familiarity with existing primitive peoples and their gods. This event was the adoption of the new god Jehovah, concerning which Moses apparently suffered none of the qualms that modern observers might expect.

It is noticeable that when existing primitive people adopt a new deity they endow him with all the general attributes of their old deity even when his primary function lies in some specialized field such as war, hunting or fishing. Migrants bringing their own god into a strange community always accept the seniority of the former god of the place, but soon invest him with the same degree of omnipotence which their own god possessed. A god may begin his career as little more than a mascot designed to protect a hunter from leopards, but if broader-minded worshippers take him up his scope will enlarge and his attributes become ennobled.

Thus we find Moses engaged in the retrograde step of learning to worship a volcano after worshipping the creator of

[6] Polly Hill, *Migrant Cocoa Farmers of Southern Ghana*, Cambridge, 1963.

heaven and earth, but apparently conscious of no disparity between the attributes of the two gods. It may well be that an earlier Israelitish band of migrants who had adopted the volcano-god and initiated their new ally Moses, had already wrought this transformation. We are told that the original character of the Arab volcano-god was that of 'a bloodthirsty demon who walks by night and shuns the light of day'.[7] Yet the beautiful benedictus which Moses is supposed to have taught Aaron at Horeb is that of a god of light: 'The Lord bless thee and keep thee; the Lord make his face to shine upon thee, and be gracious unto thee; the Lord lift up his countenance upon thee, and give thee peace.'[8]

[7] E. Meyer, *Die Israeliten und ihre Nachbarstämme*, 1906.

[8] Numbers 6:24–26. I am aware that the benedictus is considered to be a late addition to the text, but it is consistent with the probability that Moses and Aaron never attributed to the volcano-god any traits other than those associated with the God of Heaven.

# Index

Aaron, 31, 87, 89, 126, 129
Abiezer, 93
Abihu, 88, 89
Abimelech, 16, 17
Abraham, 4, 5, 11, 15–16, 21, 22–28, 31–32.
Adam, 4–5, 7
Ahab, 35, 98–99.
Ahaziah, 36
Ahijah, 98
Ahuzzath, 17
Ai, 16
Akaba, Gulf of, 29, 89
Akhnaton, *see* Amenhotep IV
Aldred, Cyril, *Akhenaten*, 12n.2
Amalekites, 93
Amenhotep IV, 12, 21
Ammonites, 93
Amorites, 16
Amran, 127
Ananias, 42
Angels, and circumcision, 25–26, 30–31; and Essenes, 110, 112; as hermits, 21, 35, 40; as holy men, 20–21; as international religious society, 21, 40–41, 105, 107; and Jesus, 108–109; as land agents, 15–19; and medication, 28, 42–43, 57–58, 62; and their names, 18, 30, 34, 42; as procreators, 20, 23, 34, 105, 108
Anna, 42
Anoche, Komfo, 75
Archangels, 41

Artaxerxes, 43
Asher, 93
Ashkelon, 94
Asiel, 49
Assyria, 9, 40
Attis of Phrygia, 127n.5
Azarias, 42

Baal, 31, 32, 35, 68, 85, 98–99
Baalzebub, 36
Babylon, 40, 44, 50, 51, 54, 56, 102
Baeta, Dr C. G., *Prophetism in Ghana*, 122n.3
Balaam, 31–33, 91.
Balak, 31, 32, 85
Barak, 92–93
Basel Mission, 128
Beer-sheba, 17, 35, 99
Belshazzar, 50n.26, 51
Bendit, L. J., *Paranormal Cognition*, 77n.9
Beth-el, 10, 16, 19, 36, 95
Bochim, 20, 33–34
Buckland, *The Universal Bible Dictionary*, 22n.2

Cain, 5
Canaan, 15, 18, 19, 29
Carmel, Mount, 29, 35, 99
Carthaginians, 26n.11
Chebar (river), 56, 57, 58
Cornelius, 109–110
Cumont, Franz, *The Oriental Religions in Roman Paganism*, 69n.6, 115

131